Radiant with Color & Art:

McLoughlin Brothers and the Business of Picture Books, 1858–1920

December 6, 2017–February 3, 2018
The Grolier Club, New York

Lauren B. Hewes
Justin G. Schiller
Laura E. Wasowicz

Edited by Lauren B. Hewes and Kayla Haveles Hopper

AMERICAN ANTIQUARIAN SOCIETY

American Antiquarian Society
185 Salisbury Street
Worcester, MA 01609
www.americanantiquarian.org

Library of Congress Cataloging-in-Publication Data

American Antiquarian Society.
*Radiant with Color & Art: McLoughlin Brothers and the
Business of Picture Books, 1858–1920*

Catalog of an exhibition drawn from the collection of the American Antiquarian
Society held at the Grolier Club in New York from December 6, 2017, through
February 3, 2018.

Exhibition curated by Lauren B. Hewes and Laura E. Wasowicz; catalog essays
and entries by Lauren B. Hewes, Justin G. Schiller, and Laura E. Wasowicz;
preface by Ellen S. Dunlap; exhibition conservation by Babette Gehnrich and
Laura Oxley; photography by Nikki V. Grdinich; editorial management by
Lauren B. Hewes and Kayla Haveles Hopper; design by Jaclyn Penny.
ISBN 978-0-692-96711-9

Cover: catalog numbers 37, 59, 151, 176.
Back cover and end papers: catalog number 192.

Table of Contents

Cat. 82. "Three Wise
Men from Gotham,"
*Mother Goose in a
New Dress*, 1882.

Preface

The American Antiquarian Society (AAS) was founded in Worcester, Massachusetts, in 1812 by the patriot printer and publisher Isaiah Thomas (1749–1831) and has become a vital research center for the study of all aspects of American history and culture. In 2013, AAS was the first research library to receive the National Humanities Medal and was recognized by the president of the United States for "safeguarding the American story."

The Society's mission is to collect, preserve, and make available the printed record of North America from the seventeenth century through most of the nineteenth century. The collection of nearly 750,000 volumes rests on over twenty-five miles of shelving in a state-of-the-art library. AAS participates in a wide assortment of collaborative projects, including exhibitions, symposia, public lectures, performances, and digital initiatives. Each book, newspaper, print, and manuscript tells a story or records an event, a life, or a moment in time—all of which wait to be discovered and interpreted by modern readers.

The Society's collection of American children's literature is full of these stories. Numbering about 27,000 volumes ranging in date from circa 1690 to 1920, the gathering of primers, tracts, school books, and picture books is ranked by scholars among the best in the world. Visitors to AAS are often surprised to discover that texts for children offer rich evidence on a seemingly infinite number of important topics.

Moral conduct, religious piety, economics, social mores, gender roles, and race relations are all explored in books for children. In fact, when a trend or a topic like temperance reform or suffrage appears in children's literature, it is very much an indication that the trend has permeated the culture. Of course, many books for juvenile readers are just for fun, but even titles with colorful pictures and simple texts can be useful guides to scholars as they explore the past.

Revealing the valuable content inside books for children is the job of the Society's curator of children's literature, Laura E. Wasowicz, who in 2017 marked her thirtieth year of service at AAS. Wasowicz has spent decades acquiring, cataloging, and working to connect scholars to the treasures contained on the pages of this collection. She began researching New York publisher McLoughlin Brothers in 1987 and has facilitated the purchase and gift of hundreds of titles produced by the firm. In the present volume—and the Grolier Club exhibition it accompanies—Wasowicz and the Society's Andrew W. Mellon Curator of Graphic Arts, Lauren B. Hewes, team up to tell the story of McLoughlin Brothers from its earliest days in the 1850s through the World War II era. The curators have used the books, drawings, mock ups, and games preserved in the McLoughlin collection at AAS to weave together themes of literacy, education, and social change with the incredible advancements in printing and communication technology that occurred during the decades the firm was in business. On many levels, they tell a story firmly rooted in the discipline of book history, incorporating details of production, distribution, and consumerism, which situate McLoughlin Brothers as leaders in the juvenile book trade.

The nuances and associations that become apparent through a careful viewing of *Radiant with Color & Art* are the result of four years of meticulous planning and preparations by AAS staff and supporters. The financial contributions that allowed this project to move forward are acknowledged elsewhere in this volume, but a special thanks is in order to Society members Linda F. and Julian L. Lapides and Richard W. Cheek, as well as the George M. Fox Collection at the San Francisco Public Library, who graciously agreed to loan examples from their own collections to augment the exhibition.

Wasowicz and Hewes produced much of the content for the catalog, with a special thank you to AAS member Justin G. Schiller for his essay, which offers a unique perspective on the dispersal of the McLoughlin Brothers archive. The Society's outreach coordinator, Kayla Haveles Hopper, and Hewes edited the text to bring it into shape for publication. Conservators Babette Gehnrich and Laura Oxley, assisted by Nancy Fresella-Lee, oversaw the evaluation, treatment, and display of each object. Staff photographer Nikki V. Grdinich and design librarian Jaclyn Penny worked with Hewes and Hopper on the production of the catalog. To these colleagues, and to many others unnamed, I extend on behalf of the Society a special thanks for a job very well done.

Ellen S. Dunlap

President, American Antiquarian Society

Supporters

Radiant with Color & Art: McLoughlin Brothers and the Business of Picture Books, 1858–1920 was made possible by generous support from the following:

The Gladys Krieble Delmas Foundation
Jay T. and Deborah Last
Ellen A. Michelson
Justin G. Schiller
Linda F. and Julian L. Lapides
Nancy H. and Randall Burkett
Richard W. Cheek
Michael Buehler
George K. Fox

With additional support from:

David M. Doret and Linda G. Mitchell
James Arsenault & Company
Robert and Lillian Fraker
Bromer Booksellers, Inc.
Donald N. Mott
Peter L. Masi
Laura E. Wasowicz
Jane R. Pomeroy
J. Christopher Collins
Hal Espo and Ree DeDonato

Supporters: Adopt-a-Book 2017

In April of 2017, the American Antiquarian Society held its tenth annual Adopt-a-Book fundraising event. This year, the Society used Adopt-a-Book to help offset the costs of sending *Radiant with Color & Art: McLoughlin Brothers and the Business of Picture Books, 1858–1920* to the Grolier Club in New York. Our fundraising goal was exceeded thanks to the generosity of the individuals listed below who all pledged to "adopt" books, toys, and prints that appear in the exhibition and in this catalog, or made a financial contribution. We thank them for their support of the Society and for helping to make this exhibition possible.

Lauren Allegrezza (Cat. 169)
Susan and Matthew Allen in memory of Martha Allen Parady (Cat. 156)
Robert and Beverly Bachelder (Cat. 183)
Georgia Barnhill in honor of George K. Fox (Cat. 145)
Steve Beare in memory of Sue Allen (Cat. 171)
John Bidwell in honor of Vincent Golden
Charles Steven Bolick (Cats. 151, 181)
Gary and Ellen Brackett
Susan Branson (Cat. 115)
Bromer Booksellers (Cat. 166)
Thomas and Gail Bruhn (Cat. 119)
Cynthia Buffington, Philadelphia Rare Books & Manuscripts (Cat. 59)
Joanne and Gary Chaison in memory of Lewis Nassikas (Cat. 197)
William J. Coffill (Cat. 113)
J. Christopher Collins (Cat. 123)
Sarah Crabtree
Elizabeth M. Covart (Cat. 57)
Carol Cunniff
Valerie Cunningham (Cat. 68)
Russell W. Dalton (Cat. 132)
Tracey Daniels-Lerberg in honor of Bailey Clough (Cat. 44) and in honor of Spencer Rian (Cat. 79)
Anne Davenport (Cat. 71)
Helen R. Deese (Cat. 78)
Ellen S. Dunlap in honor of Mason Rowell (Cat. 27) and in memory of Elizabeth Githens (Cat. 76)
Paul J. Erickson in honor of Charlie Erickson (Cat. 175)
Hal Espo and Ree DeDonato (Cats. 10, 72, 87)
Stephen Ferguson (Cat. 31)
Robert and Lillian Fraker, Savoy Books (Cat. 29)

Susan Gately (Cat. 41)
Susan Gibbons (Cat. 164)
Caroline Graham in honor of her grandchildren (Cat. 149)
Ezra Greenspan (Cat. 67)
Gloria D. Hall (Cat. 97)
John Herzog in loving memory of Diana E. Herzog (Cat. 203)
Lauren B. Hewes in honor of Laura E. Wascowicz (Cat. 165)
Scarlett Victoria Hoey and Robert Andrew Hummel (Cat. 77a)
John N. Hoover (Cat. 155)
Kayla and Thomas Hopper (Cat. 162)
Darrell and Elisabeth Hyder (Cat. 105) and in honor of Cristoph Hyder (Cat. 184)
Andrea Immel (Cat. 52)
Holly V. Izard (Cat. 16)
Patricia Johnston (Cat. 12)
Kate Van Winkle Keller (Cat. 28)
Elizabeth Kelly-Griswold (Cat. 153) and in memory of Trueworthy Ladd (Cat. 186)
Alison Kenary (Cat. 142)
Carl Robert Keyes (Cat. 75)
Marie Lamoureux in honor of Celeste Lamoureux (Cat. 25)
Peg Lesinski (Cat. 201)
Chris Loker (Cat. 118)
Carol-Ann Mackey (Cat. 85)
Jen Manion (Cat. 96)
Bridget Marshall (Cat. 80)
Russell Martin (Cat. 35)
Edith C. Mathis (Cat. 92)
Cheryl McRell (Cat. 40)
Amy Medlock-Greene (Cat. 133)
Marina Moskowitz (Cats. 65, 69)
Nancy Newman in honor of Donald H. Whifield
David Nicholson in honor of Bill, David, and Blake (Cat. 82), in honor of Marguerite and Will (Cat. 81), and in honor of Rachel and Nora (Cat. 90)
Doris O'Keefe (Cat. 182)
Mariana S. Oller in honor of John E. Herzog (Cat. 74) and in honor of Roger E. Stoddard (Cat. 19)
Laura Oxley (Cat. 46)
John and Daryl Perch in honor of Colin and Ruari Clark (Cat. 177)
Paula Petrik (Cats. 114, 161, 204)
Philadelphia Rare Books & Manuscripts (p. 46)
Jennifer Burek Pierce in honor of Kery Lawson (Cat. 146)
Mike Potaski (Cat. 154)
Jo Radner (Cats. 163, 198)
Ann-Cathrine Rapp (Cat. 129)
Lin and Tucker Respess (Cat. 190)

Marilyn Richardson (Cat. 48)
Nancy Rosin in memory of Henry D. Rosin, M.D.
        (Cats. 60, 168)
Phillip H. Round (Cat. 112)
Catherine Sasanov in honor of the AAS Creative Artist
        Fellowship Program (Cat. 62)
Justin G. Schiller (Cats. 53, 84, 152)
Caroline Schimmel (Cat. 140)
Matthew Shakespeare (Cat. 36)
Caroline F. Sloat and Colin F. S. Rothschild in memory of
        Mabel (Cat. 111)
J. Ronald Spencer
David Szewczyk, Philadelphia Rare Books &
        Manuscripts (Cats. 63, 106)
Sally Talbot in honor of Meghan Talbot (Cat. 24)
George and Sheila Tetler (Cat. 38)
Tom Touchton in honor of Lee Touchton (Cat. 144)
Alan Turetz
William D. Wallace (Cat. 13) and in honor of the Worcester
        Historical Museum and the Latino History Project
        of Worcester Committee (Cat. 137)
Delores Wasowicz
Laura E. Wasowicz in honor of Lauren B. Hewes (Cat. 77b)
Wallace Whitney (Cat. 37)
David Wright (Cat. 120)
Helen Younger

Cat. 84. *Brownie's Nine Pin Bowling Game,* ca. 1890.

Fig. 2, detail showing the shop front of John McLoughlin Jr.

McLoughlin Brothers' Conquest of the American Picture Book Market, 1858–1920

Laura E. Wasowicz

During the second half of the nineteenth century, the New York publishing firm of McLoughlin Brothers rose from a relatively humble storefront enterprise operating in the printing district of lower Manhattan to a firm that dominated the production of machine-printed color picture books on a national and arguably global scale. With its use of sophisticated marketing strategies, aggressive business tactics, and adaptation of new technologies, the name of McLoughlin should be a well-known fixture in the business history of American publishing. But in fact, the firm is mostly known for its pirated editions of famous British imprints, which formed a part of its product line. The company was much more than just a prolific imitator, however. McLoughlin Brothers produced a vibrant line of titles—many of them original American tales with illustrations by home-grown artists—that were read by thousands of children around the country. Nonetheless, little more than the basic facts about the firm have been documented, primarily in a 1928 company history and several short essays published between that date and 1991.[1]

Why is this? The McLoughlin brand is still visible and highly coveted among collectors of children's literature; McLoughlin picture books, games, and paper toys are regularly sold at auction, and higher-end pieces still command center stage in exhibitions and the catalogs of dealers specializing in juvenile books. The books are everywhere, but the history behind them is elusive at best. There are two reasons that a definitive history of McLoughlin Brothers has yet to be written. First, the firm's business records and correspondence did not survive. Though a large and long-lived company like McLoughlin Brothers would have produced volumes of ledgers and files full of correspondence, contracts, patent applications, and business paperwork, very little of those records have been preserved.[2] Second, a comprehensive bibliography of McLoughlin Brothers' prodigious production has yet to be compiled. The company published over a thousand titles in about 150 series between 1860 and 1890, constantly reissuing and repackaging popular books and shifting them between different series—an approach that makes bibliographic categorization challenging.[3]

One of the richest sources of information about the company is its surviving business library, which includes annual sales catalogs, books produced by competitors (many of which the firm pirated), and a substantial archive of drawings, proofs, and mock ups for its own books. The business library now resides in numerous collections, including the American Antiquarian Society, the Betsy Beinecke Shirley Collection at Yale University, the Cotsen Children's Library at Princeton University, the de Grummond

Collection at the University of Southern Mississippi, and the George M. Fox Collection at the San Francisco Public Library.[4] Considered together, the threads of these various archives help to weave a clearer picture of the firm's history.

Any history of McLoughlin Brothers must start with cofounder John McLoughlin Jr., whose energy and business acumen shaped the heart of the company (fig. 1). Born in 1827, he learned printing and wood engraving as a teenager while working for Elton & Company, a New York printing and publishing firm formed about 1851 by his father, John McLoughlin Sr., and engraver and printer Robert H. Elton. Elton & Company published and printed pictorial toy books, as well as comic almanacs and valentines. Between 1852 and 1853, John McLoughlin Jr. started issuing picture books on his own, announcing himself as "a successor to Elton & Co., New York, bookseller, and publisher of toy and juvenile books."[5] By 1854, John Sr. and Elton had both formally retired, giving John Jr. full control of the business. In a move that foreshadowed future business actions, John Jr. also soon acquired, through purchase or merger, the printing blocks of a competitor, Edward Dunigan (fl. 1826–1866), and he reused these blocks to further expand his own children's book line without incurring the expense of hiring artists and wood engravers.[6] This savvy acquisition and the practical reuse of the blocks suggest the type of businessman John Jr. would become.

The most complete portrait of John McLoughlin Jr.'s personality and approach to business can be found in his 1905 obituary printed in *The Publishers' Weekly*. It states that John McLoughlin was "a man of commanding personality who knew not what defeat meant. No obstacle ever arose in his path but it was in the end swept away. When he first took hold of the children's book and game business there was but little order or system. . . . The books were quaint but poorly printed and illustrated. The colors were laboriously put on by hand with stencils. Mr.

Figure 1
Portrait of John McLoughlin Jr. from *The Publishers' Weekly*, May 6, 1905.

McLoughlin introduced the then wonderful process of printing from relief etched zinc plates [i.e., chromotypography] . . . . From that time forward he led and others followed."[7] This summation serves as a guide to the business growth of McLoughlin Brothers and hints at the firm's competitive nature and long practice of innovation. Aspects of John McLoughlin Jr.'s personality recorded by *The Publishers' Weekly* —dogged, competitive, and innovative—would become vital to the success of the company. In the decades to come, John Jr. would continually seek opportunities for growth and collaboration. He copied and sometimes improved upon the strategies of his competitors, experimented with technology to enhance the illustrations in his books, and used creative marketing strategies to build a brand.

Though much of this work was still in the future, John Jr. made significant changes immediately after

Figure 2 William Boell, *View of Beekman Street, New York from Nassau to William St.* Hand-colored lithograph (New York: William Stephenson & Co., 1854). Courtesy, Museum of the City of New York.

assuming control of the business around 1854. He moved the company from 3 Tryon Row to 24 Beekman Street, a busy neighborhood full of printers, book binders, and paper manufacturers (fig. 2), and in 1855 he made his younger brother Edmund (1833/4–1889) a partner in the business.[8] Officially, however, the firm was not listed in New York City directories as "McLoughlin Brothers" until 1858.[9] During the early years of the partnership, the brothers' product line expanded from picture books to include board and card games, rewards of merit, valentines, blocks, and paper dolls. Step by step, McLoughlin Brothers grew into an empire of juvenile publishing.

Empire Building, 1858–1880

When McLoughlin Brothers opened its doors on 24 Beekman Street, many of the books being produced for the juvenile market in America were indeed as

described by John McLoughlin Jr.'s obituary: "quaint, but poorly printed and illustrated." Most books for children coming off American presses were small, printed on low-quality paper, and featured just a few rudimentary illustrations (cats. 28, 93). Printers offered children's books as a side line to their main printing business, which might concentrate instead on periodical publishing, theatrical printing, or ephemera and job printing. McLoughlin Brothers was different, focusing wholly on the juvenile market and diversifying its stock to reach the widest variety of consumers by offering multiple price points for its books.

In the early days of the firm, McLoughlin Brothers copied strategies from successful children's book publishers such as Fisher & Brother. Founded in 1834 as Turner & Fisher, this firm had shops in Philadelphia, New York, Boston, and Baltimore, an impressively national reach for the period. Fisher & Brother printed valentines, songsters, gift books, and almanacs, as well as primers and picture books for children. The firm branded many of its picture books in series with striking names such as Infantile Toys and Great Big Toy Books. John Jr. quickly co-opted Fisher & Brother's approach of arranging picture books by series. Even before McLoughlin Brothers' official start in 1858, John Jr. was grouping his titles into series at different price points, such as Pleasure Books (twelve titles, priced 6¼ cents plain, 12½ cents colored), Three Cent Toy Books (six titles, with colored covers), and Christmas Tree Tales (described as "a very pretty set of small books nicely illustrated," six titles, three cents each). After the firm became McLoughlin Brothers, the number of series on offer grew exponentially and encompassed an even wider range of price points, from one-penny books to titles costing one dollar (cat. 45). This price structure allowed the company to sell to both low-income and middle-class consumers, creating a broad market for its goods.

The firm's expansive use of named series is evident in the earliest extant McLoughlin publisher's catalog, dating from 1867. Titled *List of Toy Books Manufactured for Wm. H. Hill, Jr. & Co., 30 & 32 Cornhill, Boston, Mass. By McLoughlin Bros.*, the catalog reflects both the range of McLoughlin's inventory as well as the complexity of the firm's relationships with other publishers. The catalog includes some fifty book series, listed in order of wholesale price from the cheapest—the Young America Series (fig. 3) at one dollar per 144 copies—to the most costly—the linen-printed Fairy Moonbeam's Series, selling for twenty-four dollars per 144 copies.[10] Among the most expensive books in the catalog is *Aunt Kitty's Story Book*, likely a compilation of stories, described as having two hundred illustrations and "very showy board covers," selling wholesale at $144 per 144 copies. Along with inexpensive series and hardbound compilations, the catalog also lists paper dolls, including characters like Eva St. Clair and Topsy

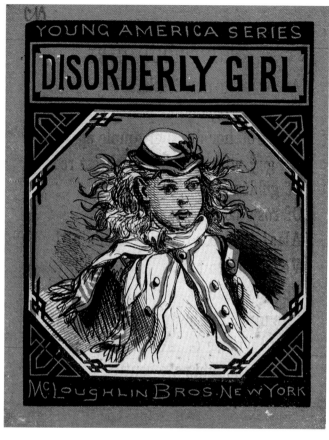

Figure 3/Catalog 44
Disorderly Girl (New York: McLoughlin Brothers, ca. 1867). Gift of Herbert Hosmer, 1978. AAS.

from *Uncle Tom's Cabin* (cat. 54), and an extensive line of sixty-five different board and card games. The catalog is evidence that, unlike most printers of the era, McLoughlin Brothers had decided to focus exclusively on the juvenile market and was capable of producing an impressive line of goods for children at a wide variety of price points.

The 1867 catalog also suggests the complex web of business relationships that would come to characterize McLoughlin Brothers for the next four decades. At first glance, the mention of publisher William H. Hill Jr. & Company of Boston in the title seems puzzling. Why would McLoughlin Brothers issue such an extensive catalog for an out-of-town firm? Furthermore, William H. Hill Jr. & Company published books for adults and advanced juvenile readers, not picture books. In addition to running a retail Boston book shop, Hill also operated a wholesale business selling blank books, school books, and stock books to booksellers, peddlers, and other merchants for resale.[11] It was in this role as a wholesaler that Hill served as McLoughlin's distribution gateway to booksellers and storekeepers throughout New England, giving the New York firm regional access to markets without the expense of a branch office, a cost-saving improvement on the multi-office Fisher & Brother model.

Further evidence of this collaborative approach can be found in McLoughlin Brothers' relationship with Philadelphia bookseller, publisher, and wholesaler Moss & Company. In 1864 two McLoughlin publications appeared on an advertising broadside for Moss & Company, and by 1872 McLoughlin issued an entire catalog of "toy books, games, &c. manufactured for Moss & Co."[12] With distribution relationships with Hill in Boston and Moss in Philadelphia, and its own office in lower Manhattan, McLoughlin Brothers had the three major American children's book publishing centers covered by 1872.

As the McLoughlin brothers were building up their inventory and expanding into new markets via wholesaling, they were also working behind the scenes, quietly building cooperative agreements with several New York publishers. In the firm's early years, they seem to have reached a gentlemen's agreement with Thomas W. Strong (1817–1892). In the 1840s, Strong opened a publishing business at 98 Nassau Street that included comic periodicals, almanacs, valentines, and picture books issued in series (fig. 4). Prior to setting up on his own, he had worked in

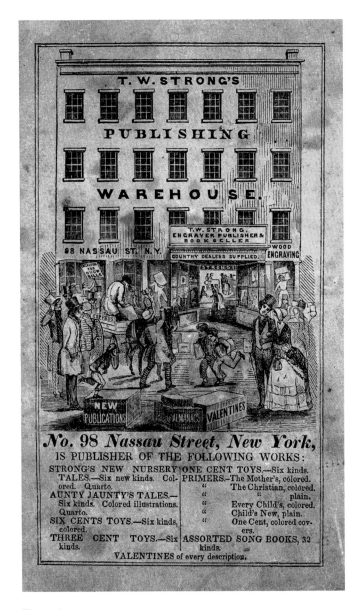

Figure 4
Advertisement for "T. W. Strong's Publishing Warehouse," back cover of *Jack the Giant Killer* (New York: T. W. Strong, ca. 1843). AAS.

Figure 5/Catalog 107
Covers of *La Cenicienta ó El Zapito de Vidrio*. Cuentos Pintados Para Niños Series (New York: D. Appleton, Co.,
publisher, printed by McLoughlin Brothers, 1864). Courtesy of the George M. Fox Collection of Early Children's
Books, Book Arts & Special Collections Center, San Francisco Public Library.

Robert H. Elton's shop at the same time that John McLoughlin Jr. was apprenticing there. In 1858 John Jr. and Strong were neighbors; it was just a two-minute walk from Strong's shop on Nassau Street to the McLoughlin brothers' establishment at 24 Beekman. In the 1860s, John Jr. and Strong served together as executors for Elton's estate, selling numerous properties in Manhattan formerly owned by Elton.[13] Then, around 1864, just as McLoughlin Brothers' star was beginning to rise, Strong abruptly dropped out of the picture book business. He changed his focus to Catholic literature, periodical publishing, and the theatrical market, eventually becoming one of the largest show printing houses in the country.[14] These facts taken together suggest that Strong reached a cooperative understanding with his longtime associate John McLoughlin Jr. to get out of toy books and to focus his attention elsewhere. In return, McLoughlin Brothers may have transferred real estate or other assets to help finance Strong's post-Civil War expansion.

Also in the 1860s, McLoughlin Brothers was constructing a discreet lateral relationship with its competitor and New York neighbor D. Appleton & Company. In 1867 Appleton, a well-established publisher with a substantive line of nonfiction, travel literature, and educational books, suffered a major fire at its 346 Broadway location.[15] This event may have led the firm to seek out McLoughlin as a surrogate production partner for part of its book line, because that same year McLoughlin Brothers printed a group of Spanish-language picture books over the D. Appleton & Company imprint for sale by Appleton in Latin America. McLoughlin Brothers used plates and illustration blocks provided by Appleton to produce the books.[16] The relationship was a productive one, and the titles issued were part of nearly fifty Spanish-language books for both adults and children published by Appleton in 1867. Although they did the printing, McLoughlin Brothers' imprint does not appear on any of the 1867 picture books sold by Appleton in Latin America.[17]

Soon, however, the relationship developed to a point where McLoughlin Brothers began printing Spanish-language versions of its own English-language picture books for Appleton to distribute. For example, *La Cenicienta* has illustrations exactly matching those in McLoughlin's Fairy Moonbeam's Series edition of *Cinderella* (fig. 5).[18] The back cover includes advertisements for paper dolls printed by McLoughlin, including "El General" and "La Señora Tomas Pulgar" (General and Mrs. Tom Thumb), dolls that McLoughlin also produced for its American customers. A bilingual packing wrapper featuring advertisements for both Spanish-language books with the Appleton imprint and McLoughlin's English-language picture books was included in shipments heading to Latin America, evidence of McLoughlin's notable self-serving promotional methods, as it used the collaboration to extend its reach into international markets.[19]

Once McLoughlin Brothers started printing Spanish-language versions of its popular picture book titles, it was only natural that D. Appleton & Company would offer those books to its customers in the United States as well as to those in Latin America. Appleton's *Catalogue* for July 1870 lists the McLoughlin Spanish-language picture books alongside other Spanish-language titles (including many textbooks) for a total of ninety Spanish-language books.[20]

The Appleton-McLoughlin relationship continued into the twentieth century. In the later period, there is evidence that McLoughlin designers and press floor employees worked closely with Appleton staff to ensure that Spanish texts were grammatically accurate. A working copy of *La Pobre Viejecita* (*The Little Old Woman*) is inscribed, "Copies to be sent to Appleton's for any correction."[21] The fact that this printing and publishing relationship lasted for nearly forty years indicates that McLoughlin Brothers was more than capable of acting collaboratively with a competitor when it made good business sense to do so.

In addition to distributing books via regional wholesalers and working collaboratively with competitors to build up their juvenile printing empire, McLoughlin also frequently repurposed its own imprints to fill special orders for non-book, commercial businesses, such as patent medicine salesmen, small-town shop keepers, and urban retailers. Around 1871 McLoughlin Brothers offered modified copies of its inexpensive (two cents each) Easy Pictures for Slate Drawing series, which were made in an accordion-fold format. McLoughlin removed its own imprint and provided blank back pages for advertisers. A copy held at the American Antiquarian Society has an advertisement for Plantation Bitters and Hagan's Magnolia Balm produced by the Lyon Manufacturing Company of New York City.[22] McLoughlin Brothers may have even provided the printing of advertisements, although retailers could have also easily arranged for printing on their own.

In the same period, a storekeeper in New Berlin, New York, sold or gave away copies of McLoughlin's *Jack and the Bean Stalk* from the Little Delights series with a printed leaf inserted soliciting the young reader to "Ask your parents to call and examine my large and well assorted stock."[23] Later in the decade,

McLoughlin Brothers printed a set of seven picture books with back cover advertisements for Vienna Flour that were distributed by dry goods merchant Thomas C. Jenkins in Pittsburg, Pennsylvania.[24] In the 1880s, during the Christmas season, McKeon & Todd Clothiers in Brooklyn, New York, gave away versions of McLoughlin's picture book *The Cruise of the Walnut Shell*. The clothier pasted a printed label with its name and address to the front cover and filled the back cover with a full-page advertisement for its goods (fig. 6).[25] Using this creative distribution model of repurposing its picture books for other businesses, McLoughlin Brothers got its titles into the hands of an expansive variety of customers with very little effort. Everyone benefited. McLoughlin was paid directly by the advertisers for books it was already printing. The retail grocers, shopkeepers, and merchants gained customer goodwill and got their commercial information into the homes of their patrons, who in turn got free reading material for their children.

Building its core business by issuing books in branded series to reach multiple levels of the market, utilizing wholesale distribution networks, occasionally collaborating with competitors, and employing creative marketing tactics was all foundational work done by McLoughlin Brothers to cultivate its publishing empire. No less important was staying ahead of the competition. The observation "No obstacle ever arose in his path but it was in the end swept away," quoted in John McLoughlin Jr.'s obituary, is quite astute. McLoughlin Brothers worked hard to keep its primary picture book competitors at bay through a variety of strategies, including undercutting prices and buying out competitors.

McLoughlin often boasted about its competitive strategies. For example, an 1872 McLoughlin product catalog proudly announces its manufacture of color-illustrated picture books equal to those made in England, but at half the price.[26] In practice, McLoughlin regularly and systematically undercut British publishers such as Frederick Warne & Company and George Routledge & Sons by printing inexpensive knock-offs of their popular books and then flooding the American market with them.[27] Around 1870, Warne, best known as the publisher of Beatrix Potter's *Tale of Peter Rabbit*, issued the popular Aunt Louisa's London Toy Books series. These books came in a large, square format in paper wrappers

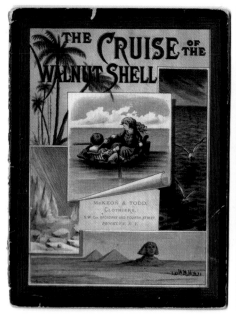
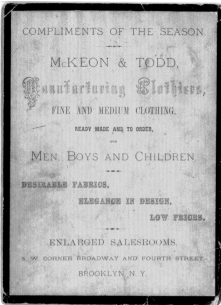

Figure 6
Covers of Richard André [pseudonym for William Roger Snow], *The Cruise of the Walnut Shell* (New York: McLoughlin Brothers, ca. 1882). With advertisements for McKeon & Todd. AAS.

Figure 7
Left: Illustration from Walter Crane, *The Baby's Opera* (London: George Routledge & Son, 1877). AAS.
Right: Illustration from *The Baby's Opera* (New York: McLoughlin Brothers, 1877). AAS.

with six leaves of text interspersed with full-color illustrations, or in compilations bound in elaborate gilt pictorial bindings. McLoughlin was quick to copy Warne's Aunt Louisa exactly, reissuing it as its own Aunt Louisa's Big Picture Books—same size, same format, same stories. Copyright laws, where they existed, were rarely enforced, and such publication piracy was widely practiced. To appeal to its primarily American audience, McLoughlin sometimes inserted titles written by American authors or illustrated by American artists into pirated series; Thomas Nast's illustrations for *Yankee Doodle* (cat. 87) and *A Visit From St. Nicholas* (cat. 152), for example, were incorporated into the Aunt Louisa's Big Picture Books series.

Because there was a ready market for them, McLoughlin Brothers continued to produce inexpensive pirated editions of books published abroad well into the 1870s. Occasionally there were

repercussions. In September 1877, the English illustrator Walter Crane (1845–1915) sent a vitriolic letter to *Scribner's Monthly* in which he attacked McLoughlin's unauthorized reproduction of his *Baby's Opera*, published by George Routledge & Sons in April of that year. He wrote, "The pirated edition, a copy of which I have seen, grossly misrepresents my drawings both in style and coloring. . . . [T]he full page colored plates are complete travesties."[28] The muted and soft illustrations published in the Routledge & Sons edition were engraved on wood and laboriously printed in color by Crane's collaborator Sir Edmund Evans (1826–1905), an exacting technician. They are elegant examples of the best color-relief printing. In the hands of McLoughlin Brothers, Evans' wood engravings were reproduced with zinc relief plates in robust shades of purple, orange, and green (fig. 7). McLoughlin offered the book at seventy-five cents per copy, less than half the price of the two-dollar Routledge edition. It is not surprising that Crane, and likely Routledge, too, was irate. The *Scribner's* letter did not have much impact on the situation, however, other than perhaps to cause McLoughlin a temporary sales slump. The offending version of *Baby's Opera* was still being offered three years later in McLoughlin's 1879–1880 catalogs, still at seventy-five cents and with the famous illustrator Walter Crane prominently named in the entry (without his permission).[29] McLoughlin Brothers continued to pirate British picture books until the passage of the American copyright law of 1891, which guaranteed some rights for foreign copyright holders.

It wasn't just the British who were affected by McLoughlin Brothers' aggressive tactics. There are dozens of examples of picture books published by the American competitors of McLoughlin Brothers in the portion of the company's library archive housed at the American Antiquarian Society, all gathered by the brothers, perhaps simply as a record of what other companies were producing, but also likely to facilitate the production of direct copies. Some of these books have handwritten editorial annotations, and others bear the telltale inked fingerprints of pressmen, indicating that they were likely used for pirated editions (cat. 103).

As the firm matured, it became more embroiled in the affairs of its American competition. On at least two occasions McLoughlin Brothers opportunistically acquired the debts of American picture book publishers, often for pennies on the dollar. It also bought out one competitor completely. In 1875, McLoughlin Brothers was a creditor in the bankruptcy of Lee, Shepard & Dillingham, the New York office of the eminent Boston firm Lee & Shepard. Lee & Shepard published a wide range of books, including juveniles such as the Oliver Optic series by William Taylor Adams and cloth-bound stories for advanced readers. Lee & Shepard books sold at price points above the core of McLoughlin's business, but its hardbound volumes still vied for shelf space with the high end of the McLoughlin Brothers line.[30] A massive

fire in Boston in 1872 impacted Lee & Shepard to such an extent that it split its business into two (Boston and New York) and sold much of its debt to its competitors, including D. Appleton & Company, E. P. Dutton & Company, and McLoughlin Brothers. With its financial health in shambles, Lee & Shepard went bankrupt, entering into a composition deed with its creditors, to whom it owed $85,259 in Boston and $61,303 in New York. This arrangement allowed the struggling firm to retain its assets while making payments on the debt to its creditors.[31] Lee & Shepard survived the process by reducing its size, but never fully regained its market position. In the end, the firm was not only less of a threat to McLoughlin Brothers' book business, it also spent eighteen months making significant payments (seventy cents on the dollar) to John Jr. and Edmund McLoughlin on the portion of the debt held by McLoughlin Brothers.

Five years later, McLoughlin competitor James Miller (1821/22–1883) also got into financial trouble and ended up relying on John McLoughlin Jr.'s financial acumen for help. Miller was the New York successor to C. S. Francis & Company, which had its roots in the early nineteenth-century Boston children's book publishing firm of Munroe & Francis. Miller steadily reissued favorites from the Munroe & Francis catalog, including *Mother Goose's Melodies*, as well as publishing maps, school books, and etiquette books. He was, in fact, the assignee during the Lee & Shepard affair, helping that firm to navigate the bankruptcy process by paying off debts with available assets and setting valuations on retail stock, stereotyped plates, and presses. Even with this experience, Miller became overleveraged and faced severe business reversals during the financial panics of the 1870s. By 1877, James Miller owed his creditors $53,000. He agreed to pay fifty cents on the dollar. None other than John McLoughlin Jr. served as his assignee and negotiated the deal.[32] After selling his books and stock at auction that spring, Miller turned his business away from publishing and became a bookseller.[33] These two debt-related events show that, by the end of the 1870s, John

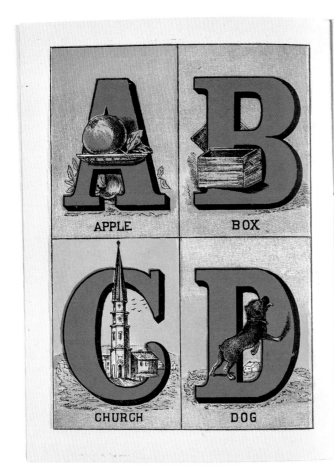
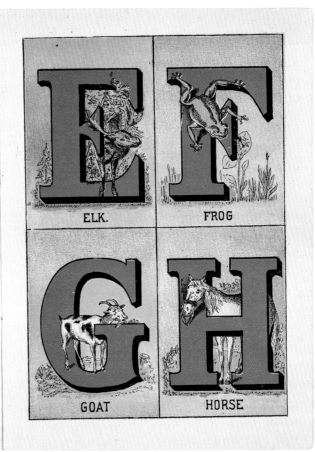

Figure 8/Catalog 105
Sunshine ABC Book (Cincinnati: Peter G. Thomson, between 1877 and 1884). AAS.

Jr. and Edmund McLoughlin had become significant financial players in the publishing world, using the fiscal assets of their firm to snap up debt and take advantage of economic downturns and disasters (such as fires) to reduce the potency of their competitors.[34]

Finally, the story of a competitor from Ohio illustrates the lengths to which McLoughlin Brothers would go to strengthen its empire. A native of Cincinnati, Peter Gibson Thomson (1851–1931) rose from poverty to found his own successful publishing and lithography business. In 1877, Thomson opened a bookstore at the corner of Vine and Arcade streets in Cincinnati, and by 1884 he had published over thirty picture book titles (fig. 8). He branded his picture books by series named for various family members, including his sisters (Aunt Rhoda's and Aunt Mollie's Series), his daughter (Mary Bell's Series), and his wife, Laura, who wrote the text for some of his picture books (Aunt Laura's Series) (cat. 110). Like McLoughlin, Thomson saw the lucrative advantages of focusing on the juvenile market, printing valentines, picture books, and paper toys under one roof. According to Thomson family historian Robert J. Buck, McLoughlin Brothers was quick to view Thomson as a tangible threat and began "a campaign of price-cutting and coercion tactics among the retail dealers, in the hope of driving

Peter out of business."[35] In October 1884, at the peak of this competitive pressure from McLoughlin, Thomson's factory was destroyed by fire. He sold his book store, and with that profit and the insurance money from the loss, reopened his production line in order to meet his critical holiday orders.

According to Buck, in late 1884 Thomson decided enough was enough and met with John McLoughlin Jr. to try to leverage a buyout, as opposed to being forced out. Thomson traveled to the McLoughlin factory in Brooklyn and made an audacious offer to buy McLoughlin Brothers. Predictably, John McLoughlin Jr. told him the business was not for sale. McLoughlin then countered with an offer to buy Thomson out. After some posturing, Thomson gave the price of $100,000, to which the publishing mogul agreed, provided Thomson guaranteed that he would leave the picture book business forever.[36] Thomson accepted and used the capital to build a new home and later, in 1893, to start the Champion Coated Paper Company in Hamilton, Ohio. The Thomson story illustrates that, by the 1880s, McLoughlin Brothers was both large and well-financed enough to make a substantial payout to swallow up an enterprising adversary without affecting its own bottom line. Mcloughlin was, in fact, at the time of the Thomson acquisition, beginning what is today considered the golden age of its production.

The Golden Age, 1880–1920

From its commanding market position, McLoughlin Brothers sustained and built up its picture book empire in the late nineteenth century by making smart use of the latest technology, linking their products to current events, and finding effective ways of marketing its brand throughout the United States. The firm's New York office was moved several times between 1886 and 1899, from the gritty shops and docks of lower Manhattan to a more genteel neighborhood on Broadway near Union Square.[37] In 1869, McLoughlin Brothers began construction

on a color printing factory at South 11th and Berry streets in Brooklyn, which comprised several buildings and was completed by 1872. This factory eventually employed as many as 525 pressmen, feeders, and floor staff, as well as 75 artists, and served as the chief site of the firm's experimentation with color reproduction techniques into the 1880s and 1890s.[38] McLoughlin perfected its use of chromotypography (the process of printing in color from relief plates) at the Brooklyn facility, using *gillotage* transfer processes to reproduce wood blocks from its archives and refining its use of relief-etched zinc plates to make illustrations that could be set with type. The brothers patented improvements to chromotypography in 1868 and in 1870, using the process to mimic chromolithography without going to the expense of changing their press equipment.[39] With the construction of the Brooklyn plant, McLoughlin Brothers became, like Louis Prang & Company of Boston, one of the few American book publishing houses that owned its own color printing factory.[40]

The capacity of the factory increased rapidly as the company adopted new technologies. After twenty years of printing in Brooklyn using mainly the relief process of chromotypography along with selective use of chromolithography for higher end products, John McLoughlin Jr. made a drastic change, outfitting a larger portion of the factory floor with new lithographic presses by 1895. In an 1890s trade catalog, McLoughlin Brothers boasted about this significant investment and the change to producing the bulk of its line using chromolithography, stating, "We are pleased to announce that we are now able to offer a handsomer and far cheaper line of LITHOGRAPHED TOY BOOKS than is to be bought anywhere else in the world. This we are able to do because we have installed one of the most efficient lithographic plants which money can procure. While we cannot hope ever to equal by Lithography the cheapness of production we have attained through our old process, we believe a demand for a class of fine goods has arisen large enough to sustain us in

WORKS IN BROOKLYN., SOUTH 11TH & BERRY STREETS.
5-ACRES OF FLOOR SPACE.

Figure 9
McLoughlin Brothers factory in Brooklyn, detail on back cover of *McLoughlin Brothers Fifty-Fifth Annual Catalogue of Paper and Linen Toy Books…* (New York: McLoughlin Brothers, 1903). Courtesy of the George M. Fox Collection of Early Children's Books, Book Arts & Special Collections Center, San Francisco Public Library.

their manufacture" (fig. 9).[41] In 1905, one report stated that "the Brooklyn factory was gradually enlarged until, at present, it is the largest of its kind in the country, if not the world," and four years later there were 850 employees in Brooklyn designing, printing, manufacturing, and delivering McLoughlin Brothers products to customers across the country.[42] McLoughlin's willingness to invest in updated printing technology, though risky, was an important factor in its ability to stay ahead of the market and is one reason for its continued longevity.

McLoughlin Brothers, while always innovative, reached the peak of its creative production in the decades between 1880 and 1900, creating beautiful and engaging proscenium-style theatrical books (cats. 168, 169), flap books (cats. 140, 170), and colorful shaped books (cats. 97, 129, 173). John McLoughlin Jr. was careful to legally protect both the format and the content of these books wherever possible, clearly branding them with the company name on the cover and often securing patents and copyrights for

the technology or design.[43] Changes in intellectual property laws and the firm's continuing squabbles with competitors no doubt encouraged McLoughlin Brothers to take legal precautions to protect its products. One of the earliest product patents filed by the company was made on July 23, 1872, to copyright a piece of political ephemera designed by John McLoughlin Jr. during that year's presidential election.[44] A constant, nearly relentless flurry of patent activity followed, as the firm continued to try to protect the company's inventions and, in an ironic twist, stave off the increased pirating of its books and games by other publishers.[45] In 1903 the company took one copyright case all the way to the Supreme Court, spending years in litigation to try and keep foreign printers from skirting newly formed U.S. copyright regulations.[46]

With its products secured by both patent and copyright, McLoughlin enjoyed a significantly stable commercial footing to invest in the production of books and paper toys with uniquely American themes

Figure 10
Game of Round the World with Nellie Bly (New York: McLoughlin Brothers, 1890).
Gift of Medusa Brewing Company, 2016. AAS.

without the fear of comprehensive encroachment by competitors. During the boom years of the 1880s and 1890s, McLoughlin Brothers produced original books and toys associated with several timely cultural events and trends. Well-known entertainers such as Tom Thumb (cat. 53) and Buffalo Bill Cody (cat. 67) appeared as paper toys during the golden years. In 1890, McLoughlin Brothers issued a board game tied into the circumnavigation of the globe being attempted by *New York World* reporter Nellie Bly (fig. 10). In the 1860s, the company had produced successful Civil War–themed products with military content (cat. 51), and it did the same in 1898 during the Spanish-American War, selling toy soldiers in modern dress and puzzles featuring the latest American war ships. It issued multiple products associated with late nineteenth-century popular sports, including board games focused on baseball, bicycling, football (cat. 183), and rowing. The firm kept up with fictional trends as well. It collaborated with Canadian artist Palmer Cox (1840–1924) to capitalize on that artist's "brownie" stories, which were all the rage at the end of the century. Cox's brownies were imaginary, comical characters that quickly caught the fancy of the American public. In 1895, Mcloughlin Brothers published Cox's *The Brownie Year Book* and in characteristic fashion made multiple brownie spinoff products, such as puzzles, picture blocks, and even a bowling game (cats. 84, 85).

By the turn of the twentieth century, McLoughlin had created an astonishing distribution and marketing network, exploiting the growing number of nationwide retail bookstores to circulate its picture books. Building on its earlier work with wholesalers Hill and Moss, the company set up an impressive distribution channel and offered multiple wholesale packages and prices for its goods, which could easily be ordered by telegraph and shipped from Brooklyn.[47] In 1895, Burrows Brothers Company of Cleveland, self-described as "the largest book store between New York and Chicago," placed an ad in the *Cleveland Plain Dealer* for "artistic toy books from the lists of

Tuck, Dutton, McLoughlin Bros., and all the leading makers."[48] Here McLoughlin was listed on par with multinational picture book publishers Raphael Tuck and E. P. Dutton of Boston. Selected McLoughlin picture books also continued to be sold wholesale by multicity outfits such as Butler Brothers, which had offices in New York, Chicago, St. Louis, and Minneapolis. A 1909 commercial broadside issued by Butler advertised the Mcloughlin line with "a representative selection of 12 series comprising the favorites—ABC and juvenile stories, in paper, board and linen stock."[49]

In addition to mail order and wholesalers, another part of the distribution network set up by McLoughlin Brothers involved salesmen who made face-to-face contact with local buyers, a step that was key to the company's success in the late nineteenth and early twentieth centuries. Sales representatives would rent a hotel suite in a given city and invite buyers from local department stores and other retail operations to come see the display of books and games and to place orders.[50] McLoughlin vice president Charles Miller (1869–1951) regularly took an array of McLoughlin games on the road during selling expeditions in this period (fig. 11). Salesman John H. Black, who was hired away from Louis Prang & Company in 1881

Figure 11
Charles Miller with display of McLoughlin Brothers games, ca. 1895. Gift of Herbert H. Hosmer, 1978. AAS.

and worked for McLoughlin Brothers for twenty-seven years, mostly during the busy golden age of the 1880s and 1890s, sometimes traveled with Miller.[51] Black's obituary emphasized how he extended the company's reach, stating, "In [McLoughlin's] service he visited nearly every section of the country, and several times went abroad to introduce McLoughlin goods to the English markets, paving the road for a surprisingly large and profitable trade there. Mr. Black . . . made regular trips through the West to the Pacific Coast."[52] These salesmen introduced an inventory of hundreds of titles to potential vendors, including department stores, stationers, booksellers, and other retail establishments. The firm continued to offer multiple series featuring their most popular tales at different price points, and as sales were tracked using inventory numbers, the company could effectively pinpoint a product's success or failure. Today this sort of inventory control is achieved through computerized algorithms and spreadsheets, but McLoughlin Brothers salesmen relied on a series of code words and numbers recorded in long, narrow notebooks that could later be reviewed and assessed in Brooklyn.[53]

In April 1918, towards the end of the golden age, an attempt to brand McLoughlin picture books was made with the introduction of a trademark titled "Educate—Amuse," which featured a pair of owls (see p. 7). The firm took out a full-page advertisement in *The Publishers' Weekly* to declare 1918 its ninetieth anniversary (a spurious claim, since the company did not officially begin until 1858). The advertisement looked back on the previous decades with pride, stating, "During this long period the firm has spared neither expense nor effort to make each of its articles a true inspiration to childhood—affording genuine amusement while formulating good habits of thinking."[54] Editors of *The Publishers' Weekly* weighed in, calling McLoughlin Brothers "America's oldest publishers of juvenile books," and noting, "Years ago, our grandfathers as boys neglected chores and curled up in hickory arm chairs to read 'Grimm's Fairy-tales,' the deeds of George Washington, 'Pilgrims' Progress,'

and other McLoughlin classics of the times. No doubt, Lincoln as a youth read them too."[55] For the first time, the firm was looking backwards instead of ahead, playing off its old successes rather than innovating with new techniques or appealing to children of 1918 with contemporary subjects. The selection of the trademark and the tie to the anniversary of the founding of the company were signals that change was coming to McLoughlin Brothers.

McLoughlin Brothers Moves to Springfield, 1920

After fifty-two years of adapting, innovating, and enjoying success, McLoughlin Brothers began to struggle in the years following World War I. In 1919, a McLoughlin executive drafted an internal memo alerting his colleagues to the chaotic state of the firm's production line in Brooklyn. At this point, John McLoughlin Jr. had been dead for fourteen years and had been predeceased by Edmund, who died in 1889.[56] John Jr.'s son Charles died in 1914, and his other son, James, had outside interests that left him little time or desire to oversee the publishing business. According to the memo, the firm's vast production plant was underutilized, and quality suffered from a waste of raw materials, inefficient resource management, and a profound lack of supervision. The writer was clearly upset by the lack of commitment to quality: "This most important factor, quality seems to have been entirely ignored during the past year and as a result many of the items in stock are far below our usual standard."[57] A good example of this decline in quality is illustrated by *The Story of a Fight* (cat. 186), which the company promoted as "unique, not only in juvenile literature but in historical literature."[58] Although featuring a well-designed pictorial binding, a chromolithographed frontispiece, and a hefty 250 pages, the paper quality was very poor and the 90 interior illustrations looked muddy, the result of using a poorly executed halftone photographic process. Without the guidance and drive of members of the McLoughlin family, the firm's ship faltered, never to

Figure 12
Plate VI from *One Hundred Years of Children's Books* (Springfield, MA: McLoughlin Brothers, Inc. 1928). AAS.

regain its dominance in the American picture book market.

In 1920, because of disinterest on the part of the McLoughlin family and the firm's inability to utilize its resources effectively, the McLoughlin name and its inventory were sold to game manufacturer (and longtime competitor) Milton Bradley. A circular to trade customers dated September 15, 1920, formally announcing the sale proclaims, "In disposing of our business to our valiant competition we are confident the line is now stabilized; is in most competent hands; and that you will be given the greatest variety of merchandise, best service, and lowest prices consistent with quality."[59] Milton Bradley bought the entire inventory and subsumed the McLoughlin games under the Bradley brand while spinning off a book line that retained the McLoughlin imprint.[60] The Brooklyn plant was closed and the contents sold or moved to the Milton Bradley plant in Springfield, Massachusetts.[61]

To their credit, Milton Bradley executives in charge of the McLoughlin line, including Charles Miller—the former vice president of McLoughlin Brothers who had moved to Milton Bradley with the sale of the firm—and George A. Fox (1875–1946), worked hard to try and revitalize McLoughlin picture books. A company history titled *One Hundred Years of Children's Books*, published in 1928, included a revised catalog of McLoughlin Brothers picture books touted as "The Centennial Line" (fig. 12).[62] A blend of old and new, the line included shaped books of animals and a version of Mother Goose first issued during the McLoughlin heyday of the 1890s, as well as some new picture book products, such as the shaped Toddle Girls' and Toddle Boys' Series. Much of the line probably looked outdated to children living in post-World War I America. By the 1930s, the company stopped printing most of the old titles and was issuing inexpensive books such as *Our America* (cat. 201), printed in contemporary designs and colors and featuring children outfitted in modern dress, along with a series of pop-up books called Johnny Jump-Ups (cat. 205). Also in the 1930s, Milton Bradley tried to maintain the tradition of linking McLoughlin Brothers picture books to contemporary trends by publishing several books linked to popular movies that featured characters from King Syndicate cartoons, including Popeye the Sailor and Little Anne Rooney (cat. 204).

Despite all these attempts, McLoughlin picture books never regained their stature. Between 1950 and 1951, amid the threat of liquidation, Bradley executive officers Charles Miller and George M. Fox divided among themselves the McLoughlin Brothers archival collection of books, drawings, illustration blocks, paper dolls, puzzles, and games.[63] In December 1951, the McLoughlin Brothers trademark was sold to New York toy manufacturer Julius Kusher.[64] Under Kusher's leadership, some popular favorites, such as the Jolly Jump-Ups, were reissued. But this was apparently still not enough to turn a meaningful profit for Kusher; he sold the McLoughlin line of children's books to Grosset & Dunlap in June 1954. After that date, just a few books bearing the McLoughlin imprint were issued, and the legal entity of McLoughlin Brothers was formally dissolved on October 12, 1984.[65]

****

In the decades between 1850 and 1890, childhood in America emerged as an identifiable cultural concept with an implied consumer aspect. The word "childhood" first found its way into American children's books in the eighteenth century and was steadily used in the writing of didactic literature advocating self-reflection and moral behavior. It was the establishment of an international children's book market with creative and entrepreneurial publishers like McLoughlin Brothers that provided the distinct material and visual culture of childhood.

McLoughlin Brothers' unhesitatingly proprietary attitude toward both its products and consumer base kept it alive and flourishing for over fifty years, a notable achievement for any business, but an especially important one in the history of children's picture book publishing. As one of the first publishers to focus exclusively on products for children, McLoughlin was able to shape and define the American picture book market. It used wholesale and retail channels to distribute its books across the country and in Europe; produced picture-dominated books, frequently in color, that significantly escalated consumers' expectations that they could get an image-laden book at an affordable price; created popular content that reflected the modern world of the child consumer; and even allowed its books to be repurposed as advertising. McLoughlin kept a keen eye on the competition and took swift action to push competitors out of the picture book business through cheaper manufacturing processes and price undercutting. John Jr. and Edmund McLoughlin were ruthless competitors, collaborating if it made sense, leveraging debt or shutting down the competition if they could, and protecting their brand through legal means whenever possible. They never rested on their success, always striving to use technological innovation to improve their products and keep prices down and profits up. In no small way, McLoughlin Brothers sold the idea of picture books as a cultural necessity of American childhood—a belief still held by most parents today.

ACKNOWLEDGEMENTS

I want to thank George K. Fox for inviting me to give the keynote address at San Francisco Public Library in 2013 commemorating the exhibition of his father George M. Fox's Collection of Early Children's Books. George K. and his partner, Dorothea Preus, hosted me during my various return trips to use the Fox Collection and I am most grateful. In addition, I want to thank the following institutions and individuals for research assistance: George M. Fox Collection of Early Children's Books, Book Arts & Special Collections Center, San Francisco Public Library (Lisa Dunseth, curator); Cotsen Children's Library, Princeton University (Andrea Immel, curator, and Jeff Barton, cataloger); Betsy Beinecke Shirley Collection, Yale University (Timothy Young, curator); New-York Historical Society; New York Municipal Archives; Brooklyn Historical Society; Brooklyn Office of the City Register; Houghton Library, Harvard University (Hope Mayo, Philip Hofer Curator of Printing and Graphic Arts); R. G. Dun & Co. Collection, Baker Library, Harvard Business School; Laurel Court Museum, Cincinnati (Larry and Judy Meyer, proprietors); Julian and Linda Lapides; Richard W. Cheek; Justin G. Schiller; and Patrice E. McFarland. I am grateful to the leaders of AAS, including President Ellen S. Dunlap, who recognized the importance of my research and provided me with the time and resources necessary to bring *Radiant with Color & Art* to fruition. Finally, I want to thank my AAS colleagues: conservator Babette Gehnrich for her expertise, clarity, and good humor; editor Kayla Haveles Hopper for asking the big questions while checking the grammatical details; catalog designer Jaclyn Penny for her creativity and contagious energy; and last (but certainly not least) my co-curator, Andrew W. Mellon Curator of Graphic Arts Lauren B. Hewes, whose wide vision, deep technical understanding of color printing processes, and belief in this project sustained me and made this project much stronger.

NOTES

1. *One Hundred Years of Children's Books* (Springfield, MA: McLoughlin Brothers, 1928). Other sources include: Michael Patrick Hearn, "McLoughlin Brothers, Publishers: 1828–1978," in *Catalogue 35: Original Wood Blocks from the Archives of McLoughlin Brothers, Publishers, New York* (New York: Justin G. Schiller Ltd., 1978), 1–5. Republished by Dawson's Book Shop, 1980; Herbert Hosmer, "Hosmer/McLoughlin Collection," *Newsletter of the American Antiquarian Society*, no. 24 (June 1979): 1ff.; Rudolph Ellenbogen, "Harry Heedless, the Parrot Girls and the McLoughlin Brothers," *Columbia Library Columns* 29, no. 3 (May 1980): 9–21; Elizabeth Pullar, "McLoughlin Brothers, The Prolific Publishing House for Children's Books," *Spinning Wheel* (March/April 1981): 52–54; Bonnie Keyser, "The McLoughlin Brothers and 19th-Century Toy Books," *AB Bookman's Weekly* 78 (November 17, 1985): 1993–1998; Dorianne Carter Ruml, "McLoughlin Brothers: A Publishing Heritage," *Heritage News* (Summer 1986): 14–17; Lee Dennis, "McLoughlin Brothers: Legends in Lithography," *Antiques and Collecting* (January 1991): 35–44; Margaret K. Hofer, *The Games We Played: The Golden Age of Board & Table Games* (New York: Princeton Architectural Press, 2003); and Amy

Weinstein, *Once Upon a Time: Illustrations from Fairy Tales, Fables, Primers, Pop-Ups and Other Children's Books* (New York: Princeton Architectural Press, 2005). While these texts provide a useful introduction to McLoughlin Brothers, they do not delve into the historical context and factors behind the firm's roots and commercial development.

2. McLoughlin Brothers was sold to Milton Bradley in 1920, at which time the entire McLoughlin enterprise moved to Milton Bradley headquarters along the Connecticut River in Springfield, Massachusetts. The McLoughlin Brothers papers and records were likely lost on September 21, 1938, when the river flooded during a hurricane.

3. Jay Last, *The Color Explosion* (Santa Ana, CA: Hillcrest Press, 2005): 115. McLoughlin Brothers rarely included dates on its books, a fact which further complicates bibliography.

4. For more on these archives see Justin Schiller, "McLoughlin Brothers Archives—A Brief Account," in this volume. Digital copies of fifty-four McLoughlin sales catalogs and price lists ranging in date from 1867 to 1947 are available via the website of the American Antiquarian Society.

5. See lower cover of *Courtship and Wedding of Cock Robin and Jenny Wren* (New York: John McLoughlin Jr., ca. 1852–1853). During the 1851 to 1854 period, Elton & Company were still issuing titles under their own imprint from the same address as John Jr.

6. Hearn, "McLoughlin Brothers," in *Catalogue 35*, 2. Robert Elton worked for Dunigan as a wood engraver, and so many of the blocks acquired were made by Elton. Around 1848, Dunigan shifted focus to Catholic publishing and was out of the children's book business entirely by 1857.

7. "Obituary. John McLoughlin," *The Publishers' Weekly* 67, no. 18 (May 6, 1905): 1286–1287.

8. In the 1850s, there were some 150 printers producing children's books in New York City. See the "19th-Century American Children's Book Trade Directory," via the American Antiquarian Society website. According to New York City directories, by 1863 McLoughlin Brothers had moved to 30 Beekman Street. It moved again after the Civil War, occupying space at 52 Greene Street in 1870 and 71 Duane Street in early 1871.

9. H. Wilson, *Trow's New York City Directory . . . for the Year Ending May 1, 1859* (New York: John F. Trow, 1858): 519.

10. *List of Toy Books Manufactured for Wm. H. Hill, Jr. & Co., 30 & 32 Cornhill, Boston, Mass. By McLoughlin Bros.* (New York: McLoughlin Brothers, 1867). The wholesale catalog gives prices by the gross, or a dozen dozen, which equates to 144 copies of each title. AAS holds a typescript of the original, which was owned by children's book collector Margaret Whitton. A similar comprehensive list of McLoughlin products appeared that same year in the advertisement section of *Uniform Trade List Circular* 1 (July 1, 1867): 104–108.

11. See Hill's 1868 broadside *Special Wholesale List of Diaries Manufactured and for Sale to the Trade by William H. Hill, Jr. & Co. . . . Wholesale Dealer in School Books and Stationery*. AAS. For a sense of the books sold by Hill in his retail shop, see his advertisement in the *Boston Daily Advertiser* (December 12, 1868): 2.

12. *Moss & Co. Publishers, Booksellers, and Stationers* (Philadelphia: Moss. & Co., 1864). Broadside. AAS. *The Catalogue of Toy Books, Games, &c. Manufactured for Moss & Co., no. 418 Market Street, Philadelphia, Pa.* (New York: McLoughlin Brothers, 1872) is owned by

Winterthur Museum, Garden and Library and is available digitally via the American Antiquarian Society, www.americanantiquarian.org/mcloughlin/1872McLoughlincatalogWinterthur.pdf.

13. "Schedule O: Situate in New York City," *The Appellate Division of the Supreme Court of the State of New York Case on Appeal, Last Will and Testament of Jason Rogers* (New York: Douglas Taylor & Co., 1900): 521. This case documents real estate transactions for lots sold to Rogers in 1867 and 1888 by McLoughlin and Strong in their role as executors. The fact that McLoughlin and Strong worked together on the dispersal of Elton's property over so many years indicates that they likely had a collegial relationship.

14. According to New York City directories (1869 to 1874), Strong assumed the assets of the "late Dunigan Bro., Catholic Publishing House," the same firm that sold blocks to John McLoughlin Jr. in the 1850s. See also Richard S. West, "Pioneer Publisher of Pictorial Paper," *Ephemera News* 27 (Summer 2009): 1, 8–16; and "Death of an Old Publisher," *New York Herald* (December 31, 1892): 10. Getting out of the picture book business did not hurt Strong. At the time of his death, he was worth about $500,000.

15. Gerald R. Wolfe, *The House of Appleton* (Metuchen, NJ: Scarecrow Press, 1981): 152. Apparently, Appleton's business correspondence was destroyed in this fire. See also James F. Shearer, "Pioneer Publishers of Textbooks for Hispanic America: The House of Appleton," *Hispania* 27, no. 1(February 1944): 23.

16. The blocks originated with George Swett Appleton, who was the son of Daniel Sidney Appleton, founder of D. Appleton & Company. George used the blocks when he published the Grandmamma Easy series of picture books in Philadelphia in the 1840s.

17. Grant Overton, *Portrait of a Publisher and the First Hundred Years of the House of Appleton, 1825–1925* (New York: D. Appleton and Co., 1925): 53. See also Shearer, "Pioneer Publishers," 26.

18. *La Cenicienta ó El Zapito de Vidrio. Cuentos Pintados Para Niños* (New York: D. Appleton & Co., ca. 1867). George M. Fox Collection, San Francisco Public Library. P.3.3.1. A cache of the 1867 McLoughlin-Appleton Spanish picture books is held in the George M. Fox Collection.

19. Packing wrapper for Appleton and McLoughlin materials (New York: n.p., ca. 1903). Private collection of Linda F. and Julian L. Lapides.

20. *D. Appleton & Co.'s List of Publications for sale by Lee & Shepard, Boston* (New York: D. Appleton & Co., 1870): 48. See also Shearer, "Pioneer Publishers," 23. Shearer notes Appleton listed 21 Spanish-language titles in 1858, 42 in 1865, 90 in 1870, 112 in 1880, 131 in 1885, and 244 in 1896.

21. See *La Pobre Viejecita* (New York: McLoughlin Brothers for D. Appleton & Co., ca. 1899). George M. Fox Collection, San Francisco Public Library.

22. See *Easy Pictures for Slate Drawing. Animals* (New York: McLoughlin Brothers, ca. 1870–1879). AAS.

23. See *Jack and the Bean Stalk* (New York: McLoughlin Brothers, ca. 1875). Distributed by J. S. Bradley's New Brick Hardware Store. AAS.

24. See *Enraged Miller* (New York: McLoughlin Brothers, ca. 1879). AAS.

25. See *Cruise of the Walnut Shell* (New York: McLoughlin Brothers, ca. 1882). AAS. Also, figure 6.

26. See *Catalogue of Toy Books, Games, &c. Manufactured for Moss & Co. . . .* (1872), front cover, where McLoughlin Brothers boasts: "Gilt cover picture books. Equal to the English, at only half price!"

27. Arthur King, *House of Warne: One Hundred Years of Publishing* (London & New York: Frederick Warne & Co. Ltd., 1965): 3.

28. Walter Crane, letter to the editor, dated May 25, 1877, in *Scribner's Monthly* 14 (September 1877): 721. The editor agrees with Crane's assessment, calling McLoughlin's edition a "shabby travesty of a beautiful original."

29. *Catalogue of McLoughlin Bros. Toy Books, Games, ABC Blocks, &c.* (New York: McLoughlin Brothers, 1880): 5.

30. "List of books published by Lee & Shepard," *Uniform Trade List Circular* 1 (May 1867): 44–48. For more on the firm see also Lee and Shepard Business Records, 1860s–1906, AAS. Gift of Charles H. Taylor, 1924.

31. "The Lee & Shepard Affairs," *The Publishers' Weekly* 8, no. 13 (September 25, 1875): 511–513; and "Lee, Shepard & Dillingham, Adjourned Meeting of Creditors," *Evening Post* (New York), September 18, 1875.

32. "The Recent Failures," *The American Bookseller* 3, no. 3 (February 1, 1877): 54. In addition, in 1878, McLoughlin Brothers was listed as a creditor for Althof, Bergmann & Company (owed $1,201.17, see *The American Stationer* 6 (February 7, 1878): 12–13) and for Hadley Brothers (owed $1,445.43, see "Trade Gossip," *The American Stationer* 6 (May 2, 1878): 6).

33. "At Auction," *New York Herald*, April 24, 1877. See also "Obituary," *The American Bookseller* XIC, no. 6 (March 15, 1883): 188.

34. John McLoughlin Jr. had sufficient financial acumen to also serve as a banker. From 1874 to 1883, he was a leader at the Morrisania Savings Bank, overseeing $204,000 in assets. In 1893, he was a vice president at Sherman Bank on Broadway, which held assets of $300,000. See *Annual Report of the Superintendent of the Bank Dept. Relative to Savings Banks, Trust Companies, etc.* (New York: State Banking Department, 1872): 212–213. See also *Documents of the Assembly of the State of New York*, vol. 4 (New York: Legislature/Assembly, 1883): 165; and *King's Handbook of New York, an Outline History and Description of the American Metropolis* (Boston: Moses King, 1893): 748–749.

35. Robert J. Buck, *Trail Blazers of the Thomson Gamble Family* (Asheville, NC: Reuben B. Robertson, 1948): 15.

36. Ibid., 16–17. Buck cites an 1887 *Cincinnati Times Star* article.

37. McLoughlin Brothers operated at the following addresses in this period: 623 Broadway (1886–ca. 1892); 874 Broadway (1892–1898); and 890 Broadway (1899–1920).

38. "Strike about Over. Work in McLoughlin Bros. Printing Establishment Going on as Usual," *Brooklyn Daily Eagle*, August 11, 1899, 14. This article records a one-day walkout of twenty-five pressmen over wages. For the number of artists employed by McLoughlin Brothers, see *One Hundred Years of Children's Books*, 7.

39. "Official Report of Patents and Claims Issued by the United States Patent Office," *Scientific American* 19, no. 23 (December 2, 1868): 365. The patent is described, "Method of Etching Relief Plates of Surface Printing." On March 9, 1870, the brothers also filed an international patent for "An improved method of etching relief plates for surface printing" in London. See G. E. Eyre and W. Spottiswood, *Chronological Index of Patents Applied for and Patents Granted* (Holborn, England: Great Seal Patent Office, 1870): 1–4. For a full explanation of chromotypography and *gillotage*, see Michael Twyman, *A History of Chromolithography* (London: British Library, 2013): 315–324.

40. Twyman, *History of Chromolithography*, 391. Twyman includes a list of publishers who also had their own chromo-production facilities; Louis Prang and McLoughlin Brothers are the only United States book publishers on the list. For examples of how McLoughlin used printing technologies, see the case study of *Cinderella* in this volume.

41. *McLoughlin Brothers' Catalogue* (1895?): 1. The announcement continues: "We still continue to use our old process where it is suitable."

42. For 1905 quote see "Obituary. John McLoughlin," 1287. By 1909 the factory employed 850 people; see *Brooklyn Daily Eagle*, July 3, 1909, 14.

43. For an example, see *Robinson Crusoe* (New York: McLoughlin Brothers, 1895). (Cat. 129). According to the cover, the shaped format of this title was patented on November 10, 1891, and the text and pictures were copyrighted in 1893.

44. See McLoughlin, John. Improvement in Fans. US Patent US 129,848 A, filed July 23, 1872, and issued the same date.

45. See McLoughlin, John. Cut Toy Figure. US Patent 397,302, filed August 29, 1888, issued February 5, 1889. Many patents for games were filed between 1879 and 1918, including patents for folding houses, musical games, and target games. The firm sometimes used assignors, including Edward S. Boynton, who filed for a fishing game (see Boynton, Edward S. Game Apparatus. US Patent 450,395 A, filed November 1, 1890, issued April 14, 1891). For patents related to printing technology, see those filed on behalf of McLoughlin by Andrew Campbell, assignor, including Campbell, Andrew. Sliding Bearer for Beds of Printing Presses. US Patent 286,997 A, filed January 19, 1883, issued October 23, 1883; Campbell, Andrew. Improvements to a Lithographic Cylinder Press. US Patent 345,669, filed December 2, 1884, issued July 20, 1886.

46. McLoughlin v. Raphael Tuck & Sons, Co. Ltd. 191 US 267. The case was argued in November 1903. For summary arguments see *Supreme Court Reporter* 24 (St. Paul, MN: West Publishing Co., 1904): 105–107.

47. See *Confidential Price-List and Telegraph Code* (1894).

48. *Cleveland Plain Dealer*, December 8, 1895, 28.

49. *The Best Toy Books on the Market* (New York, Chicago, etc.: Butler Bros., ca. 1909). AAS.

50. George K. Fox, in discussion with Laura E. Wasowicz, May 12, 2015.

51. "Quaker City News," *The American Stationer* 60 (October 20, 1906): 32.

52. "Obituary. John H. Black," *The Publishers' Weekly* 73, no. 15 (April 11, 1908): 1379–1380. Black also served as president of the national organization of salesmen, the Brotherhood of Commercial Travelers.

53. George K. Fox, in discussion with Laura E. Wasowicz, May 12, 2015. McLoughlin spelled out the code in *Confidential Price-List and Telegraph Code* (1894). Salesmen's booklets included series title, retail price, wholesale price per gross, and inventory number.

54. *The Publishers' Weekly* 93, no. 17 (April 27, 1918): 1338–1339.

55. Ibid., 1339.

56. "Obituary, Edmund Mc'Loughlin," *The American Bookseller* 26 (November 1, 1889): 518. Edmund also worked as an apprentice at Elton & Company. He retired from McLoughlin Brothers in March 1886 and ran a large real estate business in Brooklyn until his death.

57. Memorandum, possibly by Charles Miller, to an unnamed recipient, folder 1, McLoughlin Bros. Collection, 1858–1920, AAS. Gift of Herbert Hosmer, 1978. This memo is one of the very few extant pieces of evidence regarding the difficulties experienced by McLoughlin Brothers during the final year at the Brooklyn plant.

58. *The Publishers' Weekly* 72, no. 1861 (September 28, 1907): 914.

59. Circular letter, September 15, 1920, folder 1, McLoughlin Bros. Collection, 1858–1920, AAS.

60. See George M. Fox to Justin Schiller, May 12, 1980, folder 5, Fox Family Papers, AAS. Gift of George K. Fox, 2016. See also Milton Bradley's advertisement "October Book Review," *The Publishers' Weekly* 98, no. 12 (September 18, 1820): 648. Bradley states that it had "purchased publishing rights, stock on hand and all plates for the manufacture of the well-known line of McLoughlin Bros., Inc. Toy Books and Children's Classics." By December 1920, Milton Bradley was selling McLoughlin Brothers juvenile books such as *The Three Musketeers* and *Fairy Tales Everyone Should Know* for the holiday market. See *The Publishers' Weekly* 98, no. 23 (December 4, 1920): 1744.

61. See sale announcement in *Brooklyn Daily Eagle*, August 19, 1920, 5. The sellers "will accept any reasonable offer" for six cylinder presses, one lithographic press, folding machines, paper cutters, and one hundred factory tables, among other commercial equipment.

62. The 1928 date was inaccurate, as it promoted the firm's start date as 1828, the supposed year that John McLoughlin Sr. started printing, although no children's books issued under the senior McLoughlin's name prior to his 1850s association with Robert Elton as Elton & Company have been located.

63. See Schiller, "McLoughlin Brothers Archives—A Brief Account," in this volume.

64. See Fox to Schiller, May 12, 1980. Fox mentions an intermediate sale to a man named Lawton before the sale of the McLoughlin trademark to Julius Kusher, but this has not been verified.

65. Department of State, Division of Corporations Entity Information, New York State, Corporation and Business Entity Database, https://appext20.dos.ny.gov/corp_public/. The Grosset & Dunlap name is now owned by Penguin America.

DING-DONG STORIES

FOR SEASONS

TALES AND PRETTY PICTURES

McLOUGHLIN BRO'S NEW YORK

Youngster Series

PLEASURE FOR PLAYTIME

HOME

ALBUM

McLOUGHLIN BRO'S New York

Playmate Series

Fig. 17
Salesman's sample book,
McLoughlin Brothers,
1898-1900. AAS.

McLoughlin Brothers Archives—A Brief Account

Justin G. Schiller

The American Antiquarian Society has been fortunate to have a long relationship with Justin G. Schiller Ltd. of New York, a bookselling firm that began in 1959. Over the years, Justin G. Schiller and his business partner, Raymond Wapner, have helped to place significant works of children's literature at a variety of institutions. Because of his interactions with significant portions of the McLoughlin Brothers business and book archive, Mr. Schiller has a unique perspective to offer on the firm. We asked him to provide his recollections.[1]

In the 1850s, brothers John Jr. (1827–1905) and Edmund (1833/4–1889) McLoughlin took over their father's New York printing business, which focused almost exclusively on printing books for children, and expanded it to include printed paper dolls, toy soldiers, card games, valentines, and other novelties. They commissioned leading illustrators of their day, most notably Thomas Nast and Richard André. They introduced larger and more elaborate picture toy books, following the style of those produced in Europe, making McLoughlin Brothers an extremely successful business that expanded rapidly and became one of the leading publishers of books for children of the era.[2]

Despite its success, the firm's business ledgers and correspondence were apparently lost in the early twentieth century, so one way to reconstruct its peak business activity is by an examination of what was left behind in the company's print archives. The history of the dispersal and rediscovery of this archive is complex. As McLoughlin Brothers' success began to wane during the early twentieth century, the continued popularity of its games attracted the attention of game-maker Milton Bradley of Springfield, Massachusetts. The Milton Bradley Company purchased McLoughlin Brothers from the third generation of the McLoughlin family in 1920. The company's children's book line was somewhat neglected by the Milton Bradley Company, and belatedly the firm began looking for a buyer for that segment of the business in the late 1940s. With the McLoughlin brand under the threat of liquidation, two Milton Bradley executive officers, treasurer George Marshall Fox (1899–1985) and vice president Charles Miller (1869–1951), agreed to divide among themselves large portions of the firm's archives.[3] A third portion of the archive went with the sale of the McLoughlin book line, which was sold by Milton Bradley to Grosset & Dunlap in June 1954. By serendipity, my company, Justin G. Schiller Ltd., was involved in rescuing these three sections of archives and placing them within the libraries of various rare book collections worldwide, both private and institutional.

The first segment of the McLoughlin archival collection my business partner, Raymond Wapner, and I came in contact with was the portion rescued by Milton Bradley executive George Marshall Fox. Fox had joined the Milton Bradley Company in 1923, where his father, George Albert Fox (1875–1946),

Figure 13/Catalog 205
Geraldyne Clyne [pseudonym for Goldie Jacobs Klein], "Jack and the Bean Stalk," from *The Jolly Jump-Ups Favorite Nursery Stories* (Springfield, MA: McLoughlin Brothers, 1942). AAS.

had been employed since 1891. George Albert Fox, in his role as head of games, was the employee who identified the opportunity to purchase McLoughlin Brothers, then Milton Bradley's chief competitor, in 1920. Milton Bradley bought everything—McLoughlin printing plates, machinery, inventory, and business records—and moved it all from the McLoughlin factory in Brooklyn up to Massachusetts. The best games were added to the Bradley line and everything else was archived.

The McLoughlin book brand under Milton Bradley was not very successful. No popular new book series were developed and executives relied chiefly on reissuing stock titles left over from the Victorian era (though occasionally modernized). The line eventually included a group of mechanical toy books called "Jolly Jump-Ups," designed by Goldie Jacobs Klein, which had annual sales of 500,000 copies, but even this was not enough to ensure the survival of McLoughlin Brothers as a viable book brand (fig. 13).

Beginning in 1926, as Milton Bradley was struggling to promote McLoughlin Brothers books, George

Marshall Fox became interested in the history of early children's books and acquired a share of McLoughlin file copies as Bradley began to dispose of what no longer interested them. Some items, however, such as printing blocks, remained stored in dovetailed wooden boxes in basements at the Milton Bradley factory. During the New England Hurricane of 1938, the Connecticut River overflowed its banks and flooded downtown Springfield, including those very basements. George Marshall Fox saw floating wooden boxes of printing blocks in the river, quickly hired a truck, and rescued whatever could still be salvaged. Eventually those woodblocks were transferred to his family's Seldom Farm in East Charlemont, Massachusetts (fig. 14). For nearly fifty years Fox continued to build his collection, buying from such notable booksellers as A. S. W. Rosenbach in Philadelphia, Charles Tuttle in Rutland, Vermont, and Whitlock's Book Barn in New Haven, Connecticut. He developed friendships with fellow collectors Wilbur Macey Stone and James D. Henderson, which included the occasional horse-trading of duplicates.

George M. Fox contacted me and my business partner in 1977. We visited him and his wife, Dorcas, in Massachusetts several times, initially to negotiate the purchase of the surviving woodblocks from the McLoughlin archives and then to appraise his wonderful collection of mostly nineteenth-century children's books, including many picture books from the McLoughlin Brothers' business archives. These books included those printed by McLoughlin Brothers as well as books published by McLoughlin's competitors, both domestic and foreign. Fox eventually donated his book collection to the San Francisco Public Library. In 1978, we issued our *Catalogue 35* detailing and illustrating selectively 125 woodblock lots on offer, individually priced from $25 up to $1,200.[4] We then contacted Muir Dawson of Dawson's Book Shop in Los Angeles and sold him more than 1,200 additional blocks, for which they issued their own catalog in April 1980.[5]

Even after these sales, Justin G. Schiller Ltd. still had about one thousand woodblocks remaining from the George M. Fox collection, and these we had stored in the basement of our second shop premises at 36 East 61st Street in New York City. Our storage area had wooden shelves and, to avoid the chance of flooding, we placed the woodblocks along the very top of our shelves, some loose, others in cardboard boxes. Unfortunately, the unthinkable occurred: we had an electrical fire between the floor that separated our salesroom from our storage facility below. This occurred in 1980. We began seeing smoke rising from the carpet and immediately called the fire department, which promptly showed up and hosed down the basement, thus extinguishing the fire. In doing so, the remaining blocks were drenched in water, and some had also filled in with melted cardboard, which stuck to carved parts of their wooden surfaces. Understanding the need to preserve these blocks, we sent several to a printer in New England to try cleaning them after everything dried off, but it would have been a long and expensive process. The blocks moved with us when we changed premises in 1984 to 1 East 61st Street. In 1988 my partner and I decided

Figure 14
McLoughlin Brothers woodblocks at Seldom Farm in East Charlemont, Massachusetts, ca. 1977. Fox Family Papers. Gift of George K. Fox, 2016. AAS.

the printing blocks should remain part of New York history, so we donated all of them to the New-York Historical Society. The museum mounted an exhibition curated by Michael Joseph from October 27 through December 27, 1992, titled *Mother Goose in New York: McLoughlin Books and the Art of Woodcut Illustration.*

The second segment of the McLoughlin Brothers archive was taken by Charles E. Miller, who served as a vice president for Milton Bradley in the 1940s. Miller passed his collection to his only daughter, Ruth Miller (1903–1984). Between 1964 and 1968, this group of nearly 1,700 books, over a thousand original drawings (both ink and watercolor), scatterings of company correspondence, illustration blocks, paper dolls, and games were purchased from Ruth Miller by Herbert H. Hosmer (1913–1995) of Racketty Packetty House, South Lancaster, Massachusetts.[6] Hosmer was the proprietor of the John Greene Chandler Memorial Museum and Toy Cupboard Theater in Lancaster, and was a great collector of childhood memorabilia and children's books. His ancestors included John Greene Chandler (1815–1879), a lithographer and wood-engraver who produced the first printed account of *The Remarkable Story of Chicken Little* (1840). In the 1970s, Justin G. Schiller Ltd. bartered with Hosmer for a selection of printed McLoughlin books and drawings from the Miller portion of the McLoughlin archives. We had met Hosmer through our friendship with artist Maurice Sendak, who by that time we were representing. Unfortunately, there is no surviving list of what we acquired from this exchange.

These swaps happened before Marcus A. McCorison (1926–2013), librarian of the American Antiquarian Society (AAS), convinced Hosmer that parts of the collection should be preserved for future researchers at AAS. Had we realized this was going to happen, it would have seriously interfered with our bartering since keeping together the integrity of an archive is often far more valuable than the sum of its individual parts. In 1978, Hosmer donated the remaining part

of the Miller collection to AAS (fig. 15). The Society owned just a few McLoughlin Brothers imprints before this donation of nearly one thousand picture books and 760 original artwork designs. The gift also included over five hundred titles by English and American competitors that were part of the McLoughlin Brothers library. Many of the items donated by Hosmer are celebrated as part of the current exhibition and are included in the catalog portion of this volume.

The placement of portions of the George M. Fox and the Charles Miller (via Hosmer) divisions of McLoughlin archives at the San Francisco Public Library and the American Antiquarian Society, respectively, was complete by 1978. What no one realized at that time was that there was still another large portion left in storage, which had been absorbed by Grosset & Dunlap when that firm acquired the book line back in 1954. In 1997 Justin G. Schiller Ltd. was contacted by an officer of Grosset asking if we'd be interested in bidding on a quantity of McLoughlin Brothers material in one of their storage warehouses in Brooklyn. We arranged to travel there to determine if it was for us. Bottom line, it was an incredible hoard: shelves and shelves of near-mint books from the 1880s to 1900s, several boxes of original artwork, and ten massive scrap albums containing printer's proofs of woodblocks from the 1850s onwards. We were told two other dealers had also previewed the material, and together, connecting via a telephone conference line with the Grosset representative, we all participated in a bidding war. After the first dealer dropped out, bidding became more serious and the second dealer quickly doubled their amount, now well into six figures, but ultimately we were the successful buyer. I was overjoyed, but it was going to take serious time to get everything moved into our shop and properly sorted.

Along with an extensive series of McLoughlin Brothers' own copies of trade catalogs advertising its books and games production, the real prize of this remaining archive were the ten oversized albums of printer's proofs with annotations throughout by the publisher. These fragile, elephant folio-sized volumes of about two hundred leaves each included thousands of proofs dating from the late 1850s to the early twentieth century, all pasted down on acidic paper. Possibly made to serve as an archive when McLoughlin Brothers was sold to Milton Bradley and moved from Brooklyn to Springfield, the arrangement of proofs within these cumbersome books lacks any chronological order but still serves as a record of the variety of imagery produced by the company. These volumes are now at the Cotsen Children's Library of Princeton University (fig. 16).[7]

Interestingly, a quarter-century earlier, a single additional elephant folio-sized volume of printer's proofs had surfaced and was handled by Milton Reissman of Victoria Book Shop in New York. It showed serious water damage, presumably from the 1938 flood, and contained an additional 1,200 proof illustrations covering a time range from 1854 to about 1870, with images for children's books, games, and paper dolls. Reissman sold the volume in April 1972 to the de Grummond Children's Literature Collection at the University of Southern Mississippi. How or why this album got separated from the rest will never be known, nor from where it had been acquired, but such

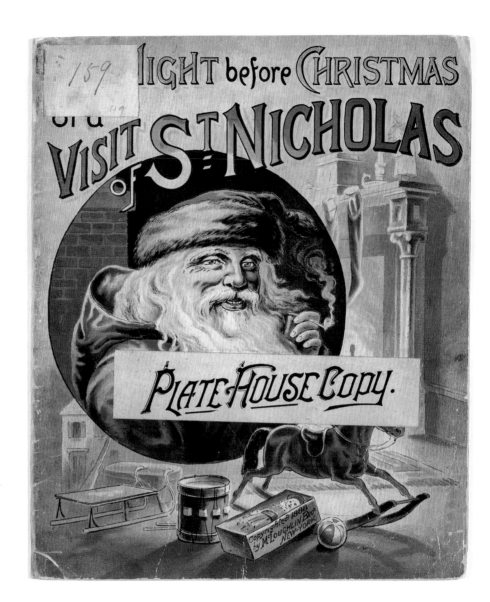

Figure 15/Catalog 153
Clement Clarke Moore, *The Night Before Christmas or A Visit of St. Nicholas* (New York: McLoughlin Brothers, 1888). Gift of Herbert H. Hosmer, 1978. AAS.

are the mysteries of collecting.

In 1997, Justin G. Schiller Ltd. also sold a large portion of the Grosset & Dunlap division to the American Antiquarian Society. The 745 items—including watercolors, pen and ink drawings, picture books, paste-ups, and proofs—joined the Hosmer portion of the archive, creating a rich resource for the study of the production of McLoughlin Brothers. The material ranges in focus from object lessons and alphabets to fairy tales and religious and hunting subjects. The material really documents the production and illustration of children's books as the nineteenth century turned into the twentieth. It includes preliminary sketches and watercolors for chromolithographs, cover designs (fig. 17, p. 32), decorative images for borders and inset illustration, as well as plate house copies, practical paste-ups, inked cyanotypes, and photographic enlargements, all used by the firm in the course of a book's production. Monies from a recently endowed acquisition fund for children's books, provided by the estate of the great collector of miniature books Ruth Adomeit (1910–1996), a collecting contemporary of Herbert Hosmer, were used to bring this portion of the McLoughlin archive to AAS.

Starting out with a belief that there were no archives surviving at all for McLoughlin Brothers, it was pure serendipity that indeed so much had been collectively preserved. In many ways, it could be said that the McLoughlin archives offer the best surviving records for any American publisher of nineteenth-century children's books, perhaps partly because it had been subdivided into smaller groups that were carefully retained. By 1997, when the Grosset hoard came to light, we could already access the

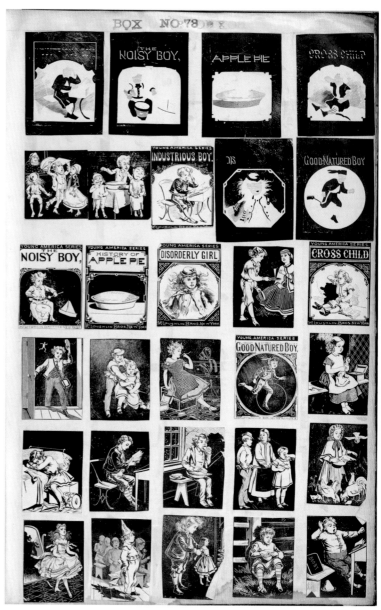

Figure 16
Page from McLoughlin Brothers publisher's archives scrapbooks, ca. 1867. Courtesy, Cotsen Children's Library, Princeton University Library.

collections that had established mini-archives of McLoughlin material, allowing us to connect them together and build upon previous discoveries. The firm's rich contribution to the history of children's literature is known to us today because of the efforts of proactive collectors, book dealers, and institutions. This catalog and the exhibition at the Grolier Club are testaments to the important legacy of McLoughlin Brothers in children's picture book publishing.

ACKNOWLEDGEMENTS

My thanks for assistance in researching and proofreading to Dennis M. V. David, George King Fox, Gregory Gillert, Michael Patrick Hearn, Andrea Immel (Cotsen Children's Library, Princeton University), Jill Reichenbach (Prints and Photographs Division, New-York Historical Society), Ellen Ruffin (de Grummond Children's Literature Collection, University of Southern Mississippi, Hattiesburg), and Laura E. Wasowicz (American Antiquarian Society).

NOTES

1. See also Justin G. Schiller, *Digging for Treasure: An Adventure in Appraising Rare and Collectible Children's Books* (Bloomington, IN: Friends of the Lily Library, 1998).

2. See Laura E. Wasowicz's essay in this volume, "McLoughlin Brothers' Conquest of the American Picture Book Market, 1858–1920," for additional details on the growth and expansion of McLoughlin Brothers before 1900. See also Wasowicz, "Children's Treasures in the Archives," *The Book: Newsletter of the Program of the History of the Book in American Culture* (March 2001): 4–6.

3. George K. Fox, "The History of the George M. Fox Collection of Children's Books at the San Francisco Public Library," San Francisco Public Library, December 2012, available via the San Francisco Public Library website.

4. *Catalogue 35: Original Wood Blocks from the Archives of McLoughlin Brothers, Publishers, New York* (New York: Justin G. Schiller Ltd., 1978). The high price was for a complete set of blocks for *Alphabet of Objects*, circa 1860, which included twenty-seven superb woodblocks comprising the cover title image and twenty-six ornamental letters incorporating an appropriate object within its borders.

5. *Catalog 458: Prints of Original Wood Blocks from the Archives of McLoughlin Bros. Publishers, N.Y.* (Los Angeles: Dawson's Book Shop, 1980). This catalog is a valuable guide to the McLoughlin blocks sold by Dawson's before they were dispersed to various purchasers, a list of which is not presently available. Dawson also created a set of proofs from these blocks, hand-printed on 475 sheets enclosed in two heavy, linen-covered folding boxes, limited to twenty-four sets, priced at $750.

6. For more on Hosmer, see his obituary by Linda F. Lapides in *Proceedings of the American Antiquarian Society* 5, pt. 2 (October 1995): 293–299.

7. Accession 5014478, Cotsen Children's Library, Princeton University. The Cotsen Children's Library was established by prominent collector and Princeton alumnus Lloyd Cotsen (1929–2017).

Cinderella Close-up: An Illustration Case Study

Laura E. Wasowicz

Readers expect picture books to be full of attractive illustrations designed to engage and enchant young readers. McLoughlin Brothers was well known for the number of color illustrations it offered inside its affordable books for children. The methods used by the firm to produce those color images are an important part of the story behind its success. A close examination of the pictures inside a selection of *Cinderella* books published by McLoughlin Brothers from around 1858, when John Jr. and his brother Edmund McLoughlin first formed their partnership, to 1920, when the name was sold to game publisher Milton Bradley, reveals how the brothers successfully adapted, improved, and developed different coloring and visual technologies over four decades of publishing.

The story of *Cinderella* has always sold well and is a fine barometer of McLoughlin's use of illustration technologies. The story, with a magical transformation, a pumpkin coach, and a fancy-dress ball, certainly lends itself to the picture book format. An 1866 reviewer writing about a newly published abridged version of *Cinderella* focused exclusively on the illustrations: "The plates, skillfully designed and painted in oil colours, constitute the chief attraction, and to children will be irresistible. . . . These pictures, so rich and tastefully designed, would be a treat of themselves to the youngsters."[1] Given McLoughlin Brothers' focus on the juvenile book market, it is not surprising that it published many illustrated editions

of *Cinderella*. An advertisement appearing on the back cover of a McLoughlin fairy tale anthology from 1867 boasts of three hundred children's picture books, including four different *Cinderellas*: an eight-cent toy book, a ten-cent toy book, a fifteen-cent toy book, and an "indestructible" (and more expensive) linen book. This advertisement reflects McLoughlin Brothers' recognition of *Cinderella* as a popular story that would sell in a variety of formats.[2] *Cinderella* was also among the titles issued in the Fairy Moonbeam's Series, a popular series of bestsellers that McLoughlin used as a pilot to experiment with more consistent and efficient ways of coloring illustrations.

What printing processes did McLoughlin Brothers use to illustrate all of these editions of *Cinderella*? In the 1850s, there were several options available in America. The most common was relief printing from pictorial wood-engraved blocks (fig. 18), which could easily be set with type on the bed of a printing press.[3] Relief illustrations could also be stereotyped in this period, a process in which castings from the original wooden blocks were made into more resilient metal. Whole pages, text and image together, of popular and oft-reprinted books were frequently stereotyped to save wear on the pictorial wooden matrices (which were costly to produce) and to reduce the amount of standing type in the shop.[4]

If colored relief illustrations were desired, there were two options. Printed sheets could be hand-colored

Figure 18/Catalog 43
Printing block for *Noisy Boy*, ca. 1867. Gift of Herbert
H. Hosmer, 1978. AAS.

with watercolors, a labor-intensive process, or additional relief blocks could be cut and the colors could be printed from them. A different block for each color was required. The illustration page would go through the press once for each color being used, and the pressman would carefully line up each strike to be sure the colors registered properly on the design. In the late 1860s, the McLoughlin brothers patented a process of color printing using multiple zinc relief plates.[5] They would rely on this method as the primary way to produce color illustrations in their books for over thirty years.

In 1869 the McLoughlin brothers took the grand step of building a modern printing plant in Brooklyn. On February 16, 1869, John McLoughlin Jr. purchased several parcels of land in the Williamsburg section of Brooklyn, just across the East River from McLoughlin Brothers' lower Manhattan shop. The parcels ran along both sides of 11th Street and were bounded by Wythe Avenue on the west, Division Avenue on the

south, 10th Avenue on the north, and Berry Street on the east. This was a substantial property that eventually housed multiple buildings, two of which were huge structures of fifty thousand square feet apiece.[6]

With the building of this plant, McLoughlin Brothers now had the space to expand production and experiment with new printing processes. In addition to relief printing, many picture book publishers in the mid to late nineteenth century used lithography to create the images inside books, and McLoughlin Brothers was no exception. In the nineteenth century, lithography relied on limestone matrices onto which a design could be drawn directly with a grease pencil or crayon, offering artists a great deal of control over the final product. The process is planographic, meaning the matrix lacks the ridges or grooves essential to other printing methods. A stone matrix is dampened after being chemically treated so that ink only adheres to the greasy drawing. This process was cost effective because many thousands of impressions could be made from a lithographic stone.

Like relief prints, lithographs were often hand-colored. They could also be augmented with single color tint stones. Chromolithography, which became the primary way of producing colored lithographs in the 1880s and 1890s, required a separate stone for each color used in the design. All forms of lithography necessitated a substantial capital investment as lithographic presses were entirely different from those used in the relief process. In 1895 McLoughlin Brothers announced that it had created an "efficient lithographic plant" in its Brooklyn factory, operating brand new lithography presses alongside its relief color zinc plate printing machines.

The following four examples serve as a visual primer for identifying the printing techniques behind the many McLoughlin faces of Cinderella. While complex and sometimes baffling to the modern viewer, identifying and understanding the different printing processes used by McLoughlin Brothers serves as a framework for organizing and dating its publications. The following examples chart the progression of the various printing technologies and coloring practices used by McLoughlin, from the water-colored wood engravings of the 1850s to the magnificent chromolithographed panoramic centerfolds of the 1890s.

EXAMPLE 1:

Cinderella or The Little Glass Slipper. New York: McLoughlin Brothers, ca. 1858–1862. Cat. 25.

With its simple design and hand-colored illustrations, this 1858 Cinderella looks like countless other picture books issued in the 1840s and 1850s. The design was taken from a wood-engraved picture book version of *Cinderella* that was first published in the 1830s by London engraver John Lewis Marks, which was quickly copied and reissued by a number of American publishers, including the Baltimore firm Bayly & Burns in 1837 (cat. 21), John McLoughlin Jr. around 1854 (cat. 24), and this version by the newly formed McLoughlin Brothers around 1858. Here, the original matrices used to make the title and illustration of dancers were also wood-engraved blocks. These were then stereotyped by Vincent Dill Jr. (1820–1906), a New York stereotyper who shared space with McLoughlin Brothers at 24 Beekman Street. The black lines of the image and the outlined border of the title vignette, along with all the text, would have been stereotyped as a single matrix, which could be easily printed on a standard press. Each page would be printed first in black and left to dry before being sent to the colorist.

Color was added to the illustrations by hand using blue, red, pink, and yellow watercolors (intentional overlapping of blue and yellow on the title border and carpet created green). Stencils were used for each color to speed the process. The colorist moved quickly and did not always carefully line up the stencils to properly fill the desired areas, a mistake noticeable especially on the blue on Cinderella's sleeves and the pink of her upraised arm. Many colorists in this period were women and children who worked by the piece, being paid for the number of copies they colored. While there are no records of McLoughlin Brothers' specific approach to coloring, according to twentieth-century Milton Bradley executive George M. Fox (1899–1985), many books produced by the firm before 1865 were colored by child laborers using bits of cotton.[7] The firm used this process of coloring relief-printed illustrations into the 1880s, even as it developed other color printing methods.

and prettiest slippers that had ever been seen,—they were

When she arrived, every one at the Palace was stru

EXAMPLE 2:

Cinderella. Fairy Moonbeam's Series. New York: McLoughlin Brothers, ca. 1863–1866.
Gift of Herbert H. Hosmer, 1978.

In the mid-1860s, the McLoughlin brothers started to experiment with color printing techniques that improved upon the use of stencils. In this *Cinderella* the colors were printed using relief blocks in basic red, green, yellow, and blue. The coloring is opaque and the application is even, unlike hand-colored stencils. The detail (p. 40) reveals layering of colors, some linear—note the red horizontal lines across Cinderella's face—and others in blocky masses, such as the red on the conductor's costume. The registration of the colors—the way the colors fall within the black lines—is fairly consistent, although not expertly done. These pages would have needed to go through the press at least five times, once for the text and the outline key and then for each color.

This edition of Cinderella is an anomaly; it looks neither like the early stenciled versions, nor like editions printed in the latter half of the decade. What were the McLoughlin brothers doing? They could have been experimenting with chromoxylography (printing with wood blocks for each color), although there is no extant evidence of the firm using this process.[8] In the latter half of the 1860s, the brothers were experimenting with relief zinc etching, and this book could have been an early attempt at that process. If McLoughlin Brothers executed illustrations using wood blocks, it must have been for a very brief period, perhaps due to the labor needed to print using wood blocks. Although wood blocks could be locked into a form with set type for printing, each color block had to be physically cut and printed separately, costing time, labor, and money. This example is a reflection of the McLoughlin brothers' willingness to try alternative strategies to mechanize color printing, the next chapter of which is seen in Example 3.

EXAMPLE 3:

Cinderella and the Little Glass Slipper. Fairy Moonbeam's Series. New York: McLoughlin Brothers, ca. 1867.

Between 1867 and about 1870 when this version of *Cinderella* was printed, John and Edmund McLoughlin were experimenting with zincography, or *gillotage*, a process that allowed them to create relief zinc plates that were less costly than wood engravings. The technique was invented in 1850 by Frenchman Firmin Gilot (1820–1872) and was used mainly for printing illustrations in periodicals, cheap books, and pamphlets. It employed repeated acid baths that ate away at a zinc plate, creating the raised ridges of a relief matrix. In November of 1868, the McLoughlin brothers filed and received a U.S. patent to improve on Gilot's process, using dustings of rosin and beeswax to strengthen the sides of the ridges. They eventually transferred hundreds of images from their archive of wood-engraved blocks to zinc plates.

To create color illustrations using zincography—a process also called chromotypography—McLoughlin Brothers created individual plates for each color needed for an illustration using the same master, a practice which simplified the color registration process. Six different plates were required for this illustration. A pink tone used for skin on the dancers was printed over with blue for the background. Plates for red, gold, and gray were also used, followed by the black plate, which produced the compositional outline and text. The dominant use of black printed over colors to tie a composition together is typical of chromotypography.

The color registration on this ballroom scene is quite good. Only the yellow plate seems to have missed the mark, resulting in the crowns and thrones of the king and queen at left printing off-register. The coloring in this process looks very different from the watercolor used on the edition shown in Example 1. The blocks of color are consistent and have a mealy quality caused by the rosined surfaces of the zinc color plates. One similarity remains, however. Green was created by overprinting blue and yellow on the curtains at right, the prince's pantaloons, and the courtier's jacket.

This method of color printing was the prevailing technique used by McLoughlin Brothers from 1870 to the mid-1890s. Lithography authority Michael Twyman has noted that McLoughlin Brothers became experts at chromotypography, which he describes as a challenger to chromolithography: "The precision and subtlety of the finest chromotypography rivalled and perhaps surpassed the best chromolithography technically, and generally its colours were more delicate."[9] Although McLoughlin Brothers was one of the most successful practitioners of chromotypography, it was also more than willing to embrace the alternative technology of chromolithography, when economically feasible, as seen in Example 4.

Example 4:

Puss in Boots. Cinderella. Red Riding Hood.
New York: McLoughlin Brothers, ca. 1895.

Starting in the late 1870s, McLoughlin Brothers used chromolithography for illustrations in many of its more expensive series books, but it did not commit completely to the process until about 1895, when the brothers expanded their Brooklyn manufacturing plant. *The American Stationer* reported on this event, writing, "[T]hey have just erected an addition to their factory. It is 70 x 100 feet, seven stories high, and is very substantially constructed being designed to carry a heavy load. It will be almost exclusively devoted to the lithographic department of the house and to the manufacture of toy books."[10] With this extension the McLoughlin plant was among the largest lithographic

factories (with five acres of floor space) operated by a book publisher. McLoughlin Brothers was proud of its expansive plant, and included an image of the factory (complete with overhead walkway between buildings) on the back cover of its publisher's catalog for 1903 (fig. 9, p. 23).

Chromolithography was being widely used in the 1890s for picture book illustration in America and in Europe. The process allowed a freedom of artistic drawing that relief printing lacked. This liberation is apparent in the illustration shown here from an edition of *Cinderella* published just as McLoughlin Brothers was getting its new lithographic printing shop up and running. The double-leaf montage of chromolithographs conveys the entire story without words, from the lonely Cinderella leaning against the fireplace to her triumphant wedding procession. The entire story unfolds text-free, deftly addressing segments of the McLoughlin consumer base challenged by limited literacy, including young children and newly arrived immigrants.

Twelve colors were used on this double-page spread, which means the sheets went through the press that many times, with a lithographic stone used for each separate color. The colors are pastel shades of rose pink and sky blue, hallmarks of McLoughlin books produced after 1890. Here the registration is near perfect. The key scenes (Cinderella at the hearth and Cinderella descending the stairs) are printed in rich saturated colors, which sets them off against six more subtly shaded secondary tableaux. This level of finesse is achievable because of the tonal nature of the lithographic process, which relies on shade and saturation, not on line, to create a composition. McLoughlin Brothers excelled at chromolithographic printing in its picture books and in elaborate games and toys created during the years between about 1875 and 1915, a period considered the golden age of its production.

NOTES

1. "Recent Publications," *The Presbyterian*, January 6, 1866, 4. The volume under review was published by Hurd & Houghton with illustrations by H. L. Stephens.

2. *Hop O' My Thumb. Cinderella. Aladdin. Sleeping Beauty* (New York: McLoughlin Brothers, ca. 1867). AAS.

3. Some children's book illustrations were also produced using the intaglio process of engraving (see cats. 4–7, 9). This process was not used by McLoughlin Brothers.

4. Standing type was type locked into a form for printing. Once it was stereotyped, the individual types could be redistributed for another use.

5. "Official Report of Patents and Claims Issued by the United States Patent Office," *Scientific American* 19, no. 23 (December 2, 1868): 365. On March 9, 1870, the brothers filed an international patent for the same process. See G. E. Eyre and W. Spottiswood, *Chronological Index of Patents Applied for and Patents Granted* (Holborn, U.K.: Great Seal Patent Office, 1870): 1–4.

6. In 1875, the property received a valuation of $20,000 in the Brooklyn Record of Assessment. See *Record of Assessment, Brooklyn, 13th Ward, 1868–1882/1886, Roll no. 26*: old page 2, new page 5, old Block 6, new Block 29; South 11th St. North side. New York Municipal Archives. The McLoughlin Brothers factory site later housed the American Book Company (1930s). See also Colin Moynihan, "The Good Life on South 11th Street," *New York Times: Williamsburg Journal* (March 15, 2006).

7. George M. Fox to Justin G. Schiller, May 12, 1980 (not sent). Fox Family Papers, folder 5, AAS. Gift of George K. Fox, 2016.

8. Chromoxylography would have been known to McLoughlin Brothers as the method was used to great effect by one of their competitors, the British team of artist Walter Crane and engraver Edmund Evans, in books like *The Baby's Opera* (1877) (see figure 7).

9. Michael Twyman, *A History of Chromolithography* (London: British Library, 2013): 322–324.

10. "New Toys, Games and Books," *The American Stationer* (August 6, 1896): 544.

48

Cat. 175.
Royal Picture Gallery,
1894.

Radiant with Color & Art:

McLoughlin Brothers and the Business of Picture Books, 1858–1920

CATALOG

Note: Unless otherwise specified, all materials in the catalog are from the collection of the American Antiquarian Society.

EARLY HISTORY OF PICTURE BOOKS IN AMERICA

The first illustrated book for children dates from the 1650s. *The Orbis Sensualium Pictus, or The World of Things Obvious to the Senses Drawn in Pictures*, was translated into English in London in 1658. It contained 150 illustrations designed to help young readers define objects and animals, understand theological concepts, and identify trades. The earliest books printed in America for children were nowhere near as elaborate as the *Orbis*, but they were similarly instructive. Early American children's literature is firmly grounded in religious subjects and was intended to be used as an aid to moral development. Few of these early titles were illustrated. Gradually, images made their way into books for juvenile readers, beginning with frontispieces and slowly multiplying to become the fully illustrated picture books that we recognize today.

The printing centers of the early colonies were primarily urban, with books produced in Boston, New York, and Philadelphia dominating the marketplace. As the population expanded across the young United States, printers in smaller towns like Worcester, Massachusetts, and Whitehall, Pennsylvania, began to produce books for juvenile readers to satisfy a growing market. During the pre-1820 period many books, including titles for children, were also imported from Europe and would have sold in bookshops next to their American equivalents.

Illustrators during this early period worked primarily in relief printing processes such as wood cut and wood engraving. These techniques allowed the images to be set on a press with type, eliminating extra work and allowing the publisher to produce all of the content for a book in one shop. Around 1780, a few American publishers introduced copperplate metal-engraved illustrations into their children's titles. Engraving is an intaglio process and requires a different style of press, paper, and technique than relief printing, and the plates cannot be printed simultaneously with letterpress type. Most engraved illustrations for juvenile literature first appeared opposite the title page as frontispiece illustrations and, eventually, were inserted throughout to punctuate the main body of the text. Both relief and intaglio printing processes were available in the United States and were used widely in book production in general, including for illustrations in bibles, almanacs, primers, and other texts that would have been seen by children. As the production of a separate literature for children expanded in the early nineteenth century, illustration took on more importance, working with—and sometimes outshining—the text.

Cat. 8. Milo Osborn,
*Come, Father's
Hope!* ca. 1820.

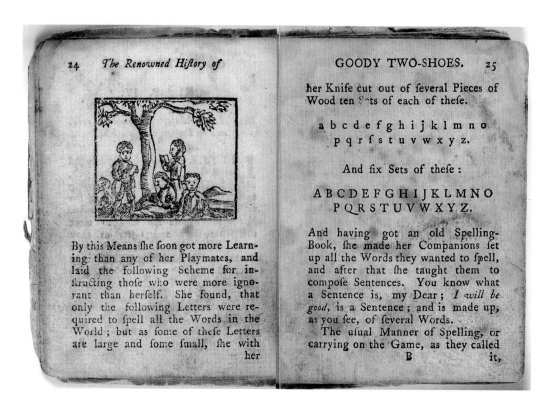

1. **"Lover of Their Precious Souls." In THE HISTORY OF THE HOLY JESUS. Fifth Edition. Boston: John Green, 1748.**

   Gift of Harriet E. Clarke, 1937.

2. **THE RENOWNED HISTORY OF GOODY TWO-SHOES. New York: Hugh Gaine, 1775.**

   Gift of Abraham S. W. Rosenbach, 1947.

3. **MOTHER GOOSE'S MELODY OR SONNETS FOR THE CRADLE. Worcester, Massachusetts: Isaiah Thomas, 1794. Second Worcester edition.**

In the eighteenth century, most illustrations in children's books were made with wood-engraved relief blocks that could be easily set with the type. These images tended to be small, as were the books themselves, and they were printed in a single color, usually black. The skill of the engravers varied, with some illustrators trained in Europe and others self-taught. A frontispiece of the author might be the only image in a book, or, if other pictures were included, they were intended to be

subordinate to the text. In the nearly fifty years between 1748 and 1794, the look of the images inside tracts, primers, and stories for children did not change very much, although a higher number of images per title was more common in the 1790s—sometimes as many as one per page.

4. **"The Bookbinder." In BOOK OF TRADES, OR LIBRARY OF THE USEFUL ARTS. Vol. 3. White-Hall, Pennsylvania: Jacob Johnson, printed by Abel Dickinson, 1807.**

   Gift of R. W. G. Vail, 1931.

Full-page engraved illustrations like this scene of a bookbinder began to appear more commonly in children's titles after 1800. Engraved copperplate images were costlier than the wood-engraved cuts that were in wide use in the eighteenth century and were printed on a different press than the text. The illustration pages (which were blank on the verso) and the text sheets would be united by the bookbinder, with each plate being

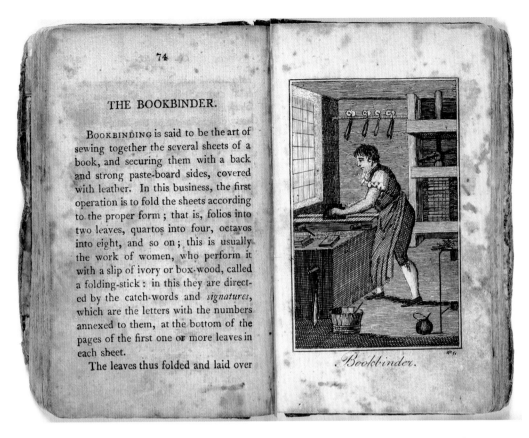

**Cat. 4.
"The Bookbinder"
in *Book of Trades*,
1807.**

placed in the appropriate signature. This volume is one of a three-volume set, with each volume containing over twenty illustrations depicting a wide variety of trades, from baker to plumber to typefounder.

5. William Cowper. THE DIVERTING HISTORY OF JOHN GILPIN. Philadelphia: William Charles, printed by William M'Culloch, 1809.

Philadelphia engraver William Charles (1776–1820) began issuing books for children in 1807, using skills honed as a political cartoonist to create charming and humorous scenes like the illustrations in the familiar tale of John Gilpin. Many of Charles's works were based on British precedents, including this one, *My Tippoo* (cat. 6), and *The History and Adventures of Valentine and Orson* (cat. 7). Initially, Charles followed the format set by earlier book publishers of setting plates opposite text,

but he eventually began to create books with both images and text wholly engraved on each page, paving the way for one of the crucial aspects of modern picture book design.

This book was printed by William M'Culloch in Philadelphia, a printer and bookseller who carried a variety of titles for children. The book sold in his shop for twenty-five cents and was one of a dozen titles offered in that price range, including *Blue Beard* and *Jack and the Beanstalk*. M'Culloch also sold smaller books for children at twelve cents each, as well as a wide variety of paper toys and games at two and three cents each. This multi-price point approach allowed books to reach a wide range of consumers and would be adopted by McLoughlin Brothers over fifty years later.

6. **J. Baker. MY TIPPOO, A POEM. Philadelphia: William Charles, 1817.**
    Gift of d'Alté A. Welch, 1962.

7. **THE HISTORY AND ADVENTURES OF VALENTINE AND ORSON. Philadelphia: Morgan & Yeager, 1823–1825.**
    Gift of Pamela K. Harer, 2011.

William Charles published books for children for more than a decade, steadily producing eight- to sixteen-page picture books full of engaging illustrations. He was among the first publishers in the United States to create titles for young readers using wholly engraved plates, meaning the image and the text on each page were printed from the same copper plate. These titles could be purchased plain (13¼ cents) or colored (31½ cents), with the watercolor work likely being done in his shop in Philadelphia. Charles promoted his illustrations as a valuable feature, calling attention in his advertisements to the "elegant and appropriate engravings on copperplate" or the "whimsical engravings" inside his story books. After his death in 1820, Charles's widow issued his popular books before turning the stock and the plates over to Philadelphia bookseller Morgan & Yeager, who continued to print from the worn and re-engraved copper plates into the 1830s.

8. **Milo Osborne after Adam Buck. COME FATHER'S HOPE! and MAMMA DON'T MAKE ME BEG IN VAIN. Engravings, hand-colored with watercolor. Philadelphia: W. H. Morgan, ca. 1820.**
    Gift of Jay T. Last, 1998.
    Image, pp. 50-51.

This pair of engravings celebrates literacy, an important part of education in America. In each image, a mother encourages her very small child to engage with "a pretty book." In 1812, a French economist noted, "The United States are more advanced in their educational facilities than most countries. They have a large number of primary schools, and as their parental

Cat. 6. *My Tipoo, a Poem* , 1817.

affection protects children from working in the fields, it is possible to send them to the school-master."[1] Picture books served as an entryway to literacy in America, allowing pre-readers to begin to formulate reading habits and understand the power of books to entertain and inform. Published in Philadelphia and sold at W. H. Morgan & Company's Looking Glass and Print Store, this pair of engravings was likely intended to decorate the nursery or parlor of a middle-class family.

9. **Mary Meeke. MAMMA'S GIFT, OR PLEASING LESSONS. Cabinet of Amusement & Instruction, no. 31. New York: Solomon King, 1827.**

Based on the success of books with engraved illustrations sold by William Charles and his

Cat. 10. *The History of the House That Jack Built,* **1839.**

successors, other enterprising book publishers began offering titles for children with engraved illustrations, including Solomon King in New York. King created a series called Cabinet of Amusement & Instruction, which included over thirty different titles, all illustrated with colored engravings. His advertisements state that his stock contained "the most approved novelties for the nursery, illustrated with engravings, neatly colored."

10. **THE HISTORY OF THE HOUSE THAT JACK BUILT. Harrisburg, Pennsylvania: G. S. Peters, 1839.**

Not all early American picture books relied on hand-coloring for augmentation of the illustrations, although that method was the most common. The rich shades of red, yellow, and chartreuse used on this 1839 publication are hallmarks of the color picture books issued by Pennsylvania Dutch printer Gustav

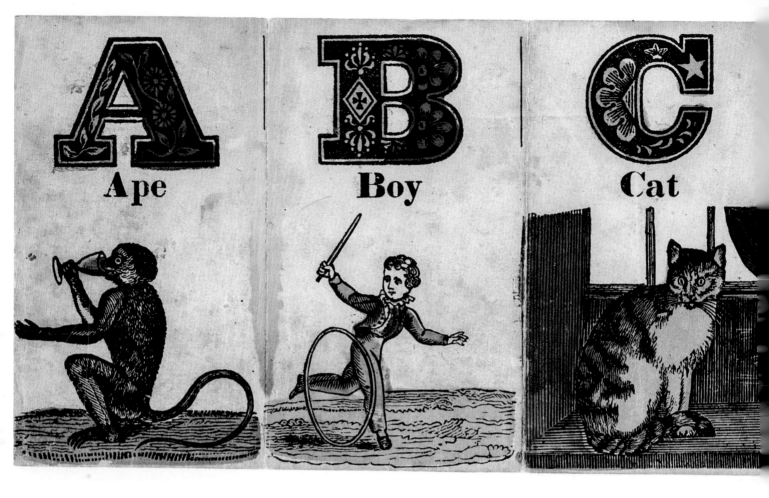

Sigismund Peters (1793–1847). Peters excelled at the use of multiblock color wood engravings in his children's titles, running his books through the press multiple times to create the colored scenes on each page. At its best, his work set a new standard for colored illustrations in picture books in Antebellum America.

11. **MY DARLING'S A.B.C.** New York and Philadelphia: Turner & Fisher, 1836–1849.

12. **CHILDREN'S PICTORIAL ALPHABET.** Strong's Mammoth Toy Series. New York: Thomas W. Strong, and Boston: G. W. Cottrell & Co., ca. 1848–1855.

Alphabet books were widely available in America starting in the eighteenth century and were often illustrated. Like the commonly circulated primers, alphabet books were intended to primarily serve an educational role, teaching young children the basic building blocks of the English language. In order to make their ABC books stand out, many American publishers experimented with the format. Turner & Fisher of Philadelphia and New York issued an accordion-style version filled with illustrations of animals and everyday objects, but designed for small hands. Boston engraver and publisher Thomas W. Strong's alphabet was for older readers and features familiar literary heroes and heroines like Gulliver and Old Mother Hubbard. The slapdash coloring on both items reflects the typical cheap but cheerful approach to the production of children's picture books before 1850.

13. **LANCASTER TOY BOOKS. No. 5.** Lancaster, Massachusetts: Carter, Andrews & Co., ca. 1828–1833.

14. **PICTURE LESSONS. Illustrations by Augustus Kollner and Morris H. Traubel. Philadelphia: American Sunday-School Union, printed by John Henry Camp, 1847–1853.**

After about 1820, children's picture books started to come in all shapes and sizes as publishers experimented with formats that would both appeal to young readers and be cost effective to produce. At just 2½ inches tall, *Lancaster Toy Books* includes an illustration showing an open book, which itself features tiny, hand-colored pictures. The text observes, "Here is a pretty book," and warns, "Children should take very good care of books, and not dirty them and tear them and turn down the leaves." Thirty years later, the American Sunday-School Union offered a moralistic plate book made up of text paired with ten large, hand-colored lithographed images bound together. This variety was a major change from the eighteenth century and prepared consumers to expect a wide range of published material for children, just as McLoughlin Brothers came onto the scene in the 1850s.

CHILDREN'S BOOK PUBLISHING IN NEW YORK

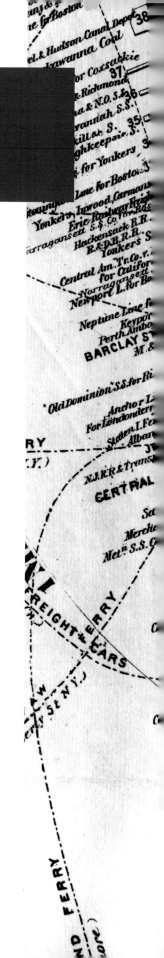

New York was a hub of printing and publishing activity when the McLoughlin Brothers firm was formed in the 1850s. The population of the city was growing rapidly, from 696,000 in 1850 to 1.4 million by 1870. At first, many printers, papermakers, and bookbinders were clustered in lower Manhattan, but they gradually moved up to midtown by the 1870s. Dozens of printers and publishers went in and out of business in New York during the nineteenth century, adversely affected by unpredictable economic cycles, failure to update equipment as technologies changed, or the struggle to distribute products effectively. Capital investment was always a challenge in the printing industry, and many publishers diversified their printing businesses to maximize the use of their equipment, providing job work services such as printing broadsides, forms, and so forth, along with book production.

There was a robust system of apprenticeships, journeyman positions, and training opportunities in the city's print industry during this period, and connections made during the early years of a printer's career often lasted a lifetime. Many printers, including John McLoughlin Sr. (fl.1828–1854), got their start on Newspaper Row, near City Hall, where vast operations for the *New York Sun*, the *New York World*, and the *New York Times* employed hundreds of pressmen, typesetters, mechanics, and printers.

Professional organizations, including the National Typographical Union, Book Publishers' Association, and the Publishers' Board of Trade, were established in this period to allow individuals to network and to create strong representation of the trade for political reasons. An 1856 statement by the New York Book Publishers' Association shows that publishers understood the need to work together: "Books, like other commodities, have their general circulation regulated by the facility with which they can be procured and the prominence with which they are presented to the public; and a judicious selection, at moderate prices, seems to be the primary requisite for a prosperous business."[2]

In part, thanks to these professional organizations, New York City provided an ideal location for the birth of McLoughlin Brothers. Dozens of trade professionals, from stereotypers to authors, could be found in its growing neighborhoods, and connections to customers around the world could be easily made using its transportation and communication resources. The city had a growing consumer base as well. Remember that population boom? By 1870 there were 208,000 school-aged children living in the city of New York—an enormous local customer base for McLoughlin Brothers and the other printers of juvenile literature in the city.

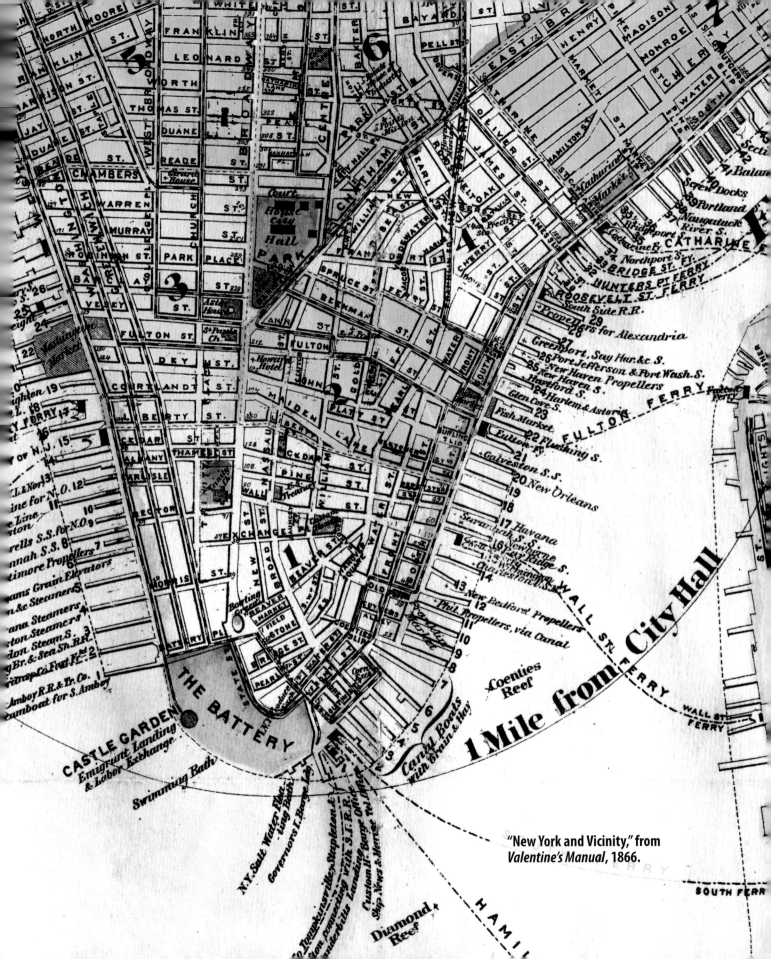

"New York and Vicinity," from *Valentine's Manual*, 1866.

15. ELTON'S COMIC ALMANAC. 1852. New York: Elton & Co., 1851.

16. THE CHILD'S OWN PRIMER, CAREFULLY ARRANGED, IN A SIMPLE AND INTERESTING STYLE. New York: John McLoughlin, successor to Elton & Co., 1852–1853.
Gift of Herbert H. Hosmer, 1978.

17. THE HOME PRIMER. New York: John McLoughlin Jr., 1854–1858.
Gift of Ruth E. Adomeit.

Robert H. Elton (1806–1863) and John McLoughlin Sr. joined forces as book publishers in New York in 1851. Both had printing experience in the city prior to this endeavor, with McLoughlin printing at the *New York Times* in 1827 before setting up his own job printing shop on Tryon Row in 1828. Elton opened his first shop on Canal Street in that same year, partnered with another printer in the 1830s, and eventually formed Elton & Company with John McLoughlin Sr. Elton & Company printed the first comic newspaper in New York, *The Pictorial Wag*, and sold a variety of games, inexpensive prints, and valentines. John McLoughlin Jr. (1827–1905) worked as an apprentice for Elton starting in 1840 and eventually took over the company when his father and Elton retired in 1854. To save funds as a young up-and-coming publisher, he reissued Elton's primers, which were steady sellers. By 1854, however, he was confident enough to bring out his own version, with larger hand-colored illustrations.

In 1858, the *Boston Evening Transcript* included an advertisement for John Jr.'s publications that emphasized both the number of illustrations and quality of color, saying, "Mr. John McLoughlin has just published two new illustrated books for children, viz *The Home Primer*, giving the alphabet in several sizes of type . . . with 48 colored engravings, illustrated with animals and scenes to teach little ones their letters. The second is *The Child's Alphabet of Quadrupeds*, quarto, giving the letters in large size with animals, colored in beautiful style. Both are elegantly printed on strong, firm paper, and sold very cheap."[3]

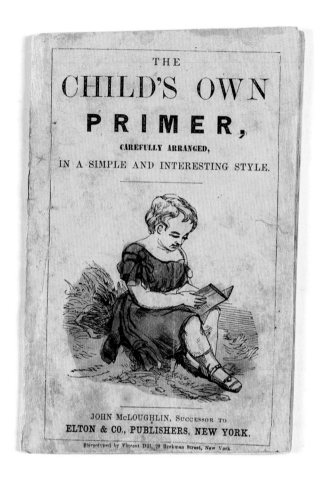

Cat. 16. *The Child's Own Primer, ca. 1852.*

Cat. 20. *The Little Drummer*, ca. 1863.

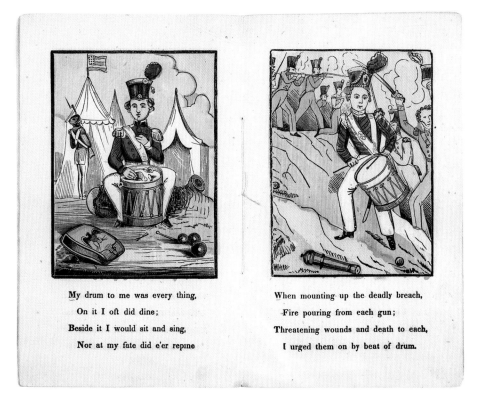

My drum to me was every thing,
On it I oft did dine;
Beside it I would sit and sing,
Nor at my fate did e'er repine

When mounting up the deadly breach,
Fire pouring from each gun;
Threatening wounds and death to each,
I urged them on by beat of drum.

18. THE LITTLE DRUMMER. Dame Wonders' Picture Books Series. New York: Edward Dunigan & Brother, 1848–1857.

19. THE LITTLE DRUMMER. Dame Wonders' Picture Books Series. Stereotyped by Vincent Dill. New York: John McLoughlin Jr., ca. 1854–1858.

20. THE LITTLE DRUMMER. Dame Wonders' Picture Books Series. Stereotyped by Vincent Dill. New York: McLoughlin Brothers, 1863–1866.

Gift of d'Alté A. Welch.

These three similar titles tell part of the story of the forming of McLoughlin Brothers. Edward Dunigan was a successful printer and publisher on Fulton Street in New York. Around 1855, he sold a number of his printing blocks to John McLoughlin Jr., who either stereotyped them or reused them to create very similar books. *The Little Drummer* was among the first titles printed by John McLoughlin Jr. after taking over the shop of Elton & Company in the early 1850s. His version of the book features hand-colored illustrations throughout and reflects his early practice of putting color on every page.

John's brother Edmund (1833/4–1889) joined the firm in 1855, and by 1858 they were listing themselves as McLoughlin Brothers in the city directories. Five years later, around 1863, McLoughlin Brothers issued a new version of *The Little Drummer* using the very same illustrations but with even more color. This version sold for $4.50 per gross (144 copies) wholesale, or about ⅓ of a cent each. By reusing Dunigan's plates and improving the images with color, the McLoughlin brothers easily created a stock item that could be sold continuously and cheaply and still be profitable.

21. **C**INDERLLLA **[sic], OR** T**HE** L**ITTLE** G**LASS** S**LIPPER.
Coloured Toys Series. Baltimore: Bayly & Burns,
1837.**

22. **C**INDERELLA**, OR** T**HE** L**ITTLE** G**LASS** S**LIPPER.**
**Marks' Toy Books Series. Albany: E. H. Pease & Co.,
1847–1853.**

23. **C**INDERELLA**, OR** T**HE** L**ITTLE** G**LASS** S**LIPPER. New
York: Edward Dunigan and Brother, 1848–1857.**
*Gift of Susan Pike Corcoran in honor of her Pike and Wright
ancestors, 2016.*

24. **C**INDERELLA **OR** T**HE** G**LASS** S**LIPPER. New York:
John McLoughlin Jr., ca. 1854–1858.**

25. **C**INDERELLA **OR** T**HE** G**LASS** S**LIPPER. New York:
McLoughlin Brothers, ca. 1858–1862.**
Gift of Charles Henry Taylor.
Image, p. 43.

Viewed together, the *Cinderella* books in this grouping reveal
how much copying and reuse was going on in the picture
book business before the Civil War. All are based on an edition
of the fairy tale originally issued by English engraver John
Lewis Marks in the 1830s, which in short order was copied by
Baltimore publisher Bayly & Burns and later by Erastus H. Pease
of Albany. *Cinderella* was one of the first picture books issued
by John McLoughlin Jr. after he took over Elton & Company. He
used the blocks originally owned by his contemporary Edward
Dunigan in the 1840s, but the young McLoughlin made sure
that every illustration had multiple colors. McLoughlin Brothers
issued another printing of the same images and story in 1858
shortly after John and his brother Edmund established their
partnership.

26. **F**AIRY **T**ALES**, OR** B**OOK OF** F**UN AND** D**ITTIES.** T**HE
B**OY**'S** O**WN** B**OOK OF** F**UN. Illustrations by John
H. Manning. New York: Thomas W. Strong, 1852–
1866.**
Gift of Charles Henry Taylor.

27. **G**RANDMA **C**HEERLY**'S** S**TORIES FOR THE** N**URSERY.
New York: Thomas W. Strong, 1864.**
Gift of Herbert H. Hosmer, 1978.

GRANDMA CHEERLY'S STORIES
FOR THE NURSERY.

PUBLISHED BY
T. W. STRONG,
No. 98 Nassau Street, New York.

Cat. 27. *Grandma Cheerly's Stories for the Nursery*, 1864.

Around 1840, Thomas W. Strong (1817–1892) and John McLoughlin Jr. were both working at Robert H. Elton's printing shop on Nassau Street in New York City. John Jr. was an apprentice while Strong was likely a journeyman, preparing to open his own business, which he did around 1842. By the 1850s, Strong was publishing a number of picture books for children as one part of his busy printing enterprise that included broadsides, almanacs, valentines, and books for all ages. Strong was a savvy businessman and ran a diversified business while also investing in New York real estate. Not only did he reissue popular titles from Elton's stock for over a decade, including the *Boy's Own Book of Fun*, he also offered an extensive catalog of new and varied types of printings. For example, in 1864 Strong published this shaped book of Mother Goose rhymes, as well as a political cartoon poking fun at presidential candidates and a Spanish-language edition of Dr. Hollick's *Matrimonial Guide*.

28. Cock Robin. Infantile Toy Books Series. New York and Philadelphia: Turner & Fisher, ca. 1850–1861.

29. The Story of Poor Cock Robin. Lithograph, hand-colored. New York and Hartford, Connecticut: E. C. Kellogg, and Buffalo, New York: Ensign, Thayer & Co., ca. 1852.

With offices in New York, Philadelphia, Boston, and Baltimore, Turner & Fisher published numerous cheap picture books with a national distribution. Its New York office competed directly with Elton & Company, John McLoughlin Jr., and eventually McLoughlin Brothers. The firm was established in 1835 and an 1844 advertisement listed its specialties as "Almanacks, Toy and Song Books, and colored Prints."[4] It also published games for children and adults as well as plays and a periodical focused on the theatrical world. Turner & Fisher's edition of the nursery rhyme *Cock Robin*, featuring a yellow paper cover decorated with a simple design of the fallen Cock, is typical of its work for children. It was likely designed for small hands, although the tale inside would require the skills of a primary school reader. A lithograph published in New York and Hartford shows three children perfectly engrossed in reading *Cock Robin*. The book in the boy's hand is the same scale and shape as the Turner & Fisher copy.

30. Dominique C. Fabronius. Fairy Tales. Lithograph. Boston: John H. Bufford, 1856–1866.

Gift of Charles H. Taylor.

In the 1850s, as John McLoughlin Jr. was starting his firm, the demand for books for children was on the rise. Very young children, like the one shown in this lithograph, were encouraged to pore over picture books as a way to build a foundation for literacy and moral development. Books such as *Reading without Tears* (1857) and *Little Lessons for Little Folks* (1861) instructed parents not only to read to their children and to have their children read to them, but also to allow youngsters to experience books on their own. This movement opened up the market for picture books where images engaged both pre-readers and emerging readers.

31. Amusing Addition. New York: John Q. Preble, 1851–1865.

John Q. Preble (fl. 1850–1890) issued nearly forty titles for children starting in 1851, including this poem designed to help readers with mathematics. His books for children included educational and religious titles, as well as natural history topics and poetry. The books he printed were really just a side business, however, as Preble's main focus was on the production of stationery, especially envelopes. In 1856 he was turning out one million envelopes each week, and in 1863 he filed for a patent related to the mechanized production of envelopes. Later in life he would own a blank book manufactory in Saugerties, New York, and a rolling mill in Findlay, Ohio.

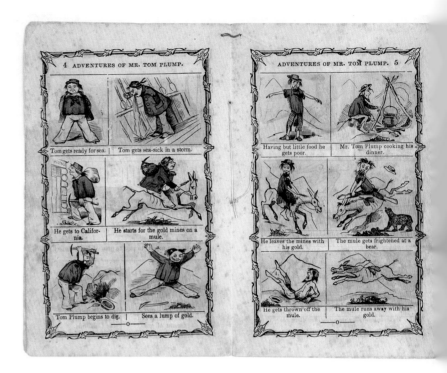

Cat. 32. *The Adventures of Mr. Tom Plump*, ca. 1855.

32. The Adventures of Mr. Tom Plump. New York: Philip J. Cozans, ca. 1855–1861.

33. Little Eva, the Flower of the South. Aunt Mary's Picture Book Series. New York: Philip J. Cozans, ca. 1855–1861.

Gift of Ruth E. Adomeit.

Picture book publishers in New York in the 1850s often reissued familiar nursery rhymes, ABC books, and religious subjects for children, many copied from European precedents. Philip J. Cozans (fl. 1850–1867), who kept a shop on Nassau Street until 1867, also offered a number of original American subjects. These include a multipaneled story book about a man who travels to California in search of gold and a children's picture book very loosely based on Harriet Beecher Stowe's *Uncle Tom's Cabin, or Life Among the Lowly*. The first sports three rows of individually captioned pictures per page, each image dashed with a few colors. The second tells the story of Little Eva from Alabama who teaches her family's slaves how to read. Cozans also published original titles focused on the events of the American Revolution,

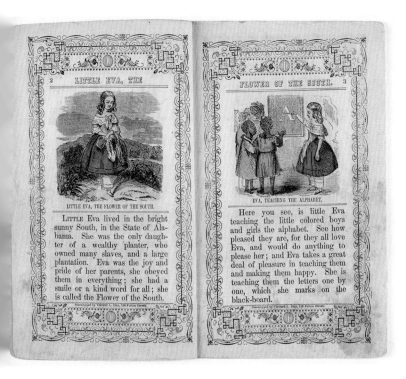

Cat. 33. *Little Eva, the Flower of the South*, ca. 1855.

a biography of Pocahontas, and a songster promoting the candidacy of John Frémont. In 1856, he was selling fifty-one different lines of "low-priced books, mainly juveniles and songsters." His inventory that year was estimated at 15,646 volumes and was valued at $1,602.[5]

34. THE FLIGHT OF ELIZA. Lithograph, hand-colored. New York: Nathaniel Currier, 1852–1856.

Gift of John Zak, 2014.

Publishers of children's picture books in New York would have been surrounded by a myriad of shops, stores, warehouses, and factories producing all kinds of printed goods, from ephemera to decorative prints. One of the principal printers in the city was Nathaniel Currier (1813–1888), who opened his lithography shop in 1835 at the age of twenty-two. He started out as a job printer, pulling music, forms, and book illustrations from his press. After 1840, he narrowed his production to framing prints,

such as this image drawn from Harriet Beecher Stowe's bestselling novel, *Uncle Tom's Cabin, or Life Among the Lowly*. While Currier, who later formed Currier & Ives, never published children's literature, the firm's presence in New York contributed to that city's prominence as a hub of American printing and publishing.

35. Augustus Kollner. VALUABLE BOOKS FOR CHILDREN AND YOUTH. Philadelphia: American Sunday-School Union, ca. 1850.

The American Sunday-School Union (ASSU) was one of the leading publishers for children in the country before the Civil War. They printed thousands of tracts, moral tales, and primers for distribution to young readers. With offices in New York, Philadelphia, Boston, Saint Louis, Louisville, and Rochester, the ASSU had a truly national reach that included individual consumers and Sunday schools open to children of all races and economic levels. The organization was one of the early adopters of the emerging technology of lithography, using lithographed maps and illustrations inside books for children as early as 1829. This advertisement for the German-American lithographer Augustus Kollner (1813–1906) of Philadelphia promotes his work for the ASSU. His earliest images for the American Sunday-School Union date to 1841, and he worked extensively as an illustrator for the organization until about 1860.

Early Days of McLoughlin Brothers

When McLoughlin Brothers began publishing, the partners, John Jr. and Edmund, made several key decisions that would set them apart from their competition. First, they committed to continuing John Jr.'s efforts to include as much color as possible in most of their books, even the inexpensive titles. This caused one newspaper editor to comment on the firm's 1866 edition of *Old Mother Hubbard and Her Dog*, "We are pleased to see that Mother Hubbard is as sprightly and active as when we first made that august old lady's acquaintance twenty years ago, except she has taken to paint. This is a decided improvement, and the illustrations of these books are well colored and deserving of commendation."[6]

The brothers also chose to issue the majority of their titles in series. Even as early as the 1850s, they saw the advantages of offering the same stories in different formats and at varied price points. Popular rhymes and tales like *Mother Goose* and *Cinderella* came in penny editions and dollar editions. Each series was sold at a particular price point, allowing the company to reuse printing plates and designs in different sizes, bindings, and with judicious use of color or without. Over the years, McLoughlin Brothers would continually repackage series, changing the name of the series or titles offered in it, and push the books out as "new" to its wholesale markets. This approach created an enormous catalog of books on offer, even though many were repackaged or resized editions. This efficiency allowed the firm the opportunity to create original content and to expand its toy line, all while selling books to distributors who could offer them to the widest possible market, from low-income residents of the tenements in New York to middle-class families in Brooklyn and beyond.

Finally, the McLoughlin brothers decided to only sell material (books, games, toys) produced for the juvenile market. In this they were unusual. A survey of titles being promoted by 128 different New York booksellers in 1856, just as the brothers were about to launch their partnership, reveals that only fifteen other publishers listed children's books as part of their core business.[7] Certainly more than that were printing books for young readers, but when describing their stock for their colleagues, only 12 percent included juvenile or toy books as part of their focus, and all of those published other kinds of books, including novels, religious texts, or science books for adult readers. McLoughlin Brothers produced valentines for the seasonal February markets, but other than that, 100 percent of its products were intended for children.

cLOUGHLIN BROTHERS,
PUBLISHERS OF
BOOKS, GAMES, &c.,
NEW YORK.

...Y'S SERIES.

...HYMES.
...S RHYMES.
...OOK.
...BOY.
...D THE OUTLAW.
...OR ROBIN
...ING HOOD.
...EAN STALK.
...ONDERFUL LAMP.
...E FORTY THIEVES
...E BEAST.
...ECTURE.

...JUVENILES.

...YS BOOK
...RLS BOOK.
...S.
...G FRIENDS.
...NGE
...N SHORT WORDS.
... OF EUROPE.
...STORIES.

Colored.

...CHILD'S SERIES.

...S.
...KITTENS. X
...RD.
...RHYMES.
...HENNY PENNY.

...OR'S SERIES.

...D CARRION CROW.

...PIPER'S SON.

Aunt Fanny's Fairy Tales.

FAIR ONE WITH GOLDEN LOCKS.
THE WHITE CAT.
PRINCESS ROSETTA.
THE YELLOW DWARF.
BLUE BIRD.
RIDDLE BOOK.
PUSS IN BOOTS.
GULLIVER'S TRAVELS.
JACK THE GIANT KILLER
REINEKE THE FOX
BLUE BEARD.
MOTHER GOOSE

Colored.

Aunt Mary's Little Series.

HARRY HEEDLESS.
ONE, TWO, BUCKLE MY SHOE.
FIVE LITTLE PIGS.
MISCHIEVOUS BOY.
GREEDY GEORGE
PRIMER
THE CROOKED MAN and other Rhymes
PETER WHITE, and other Rhymes.
JACK SPRATT, and other Rhymes.
TOM TUCKER, and other Rhymes.
OLD MOTHER HUBBARD.

Plain. **Colored.**

Aunt Jenny's Musical Series.

THE THREE BLIND MICE. X
LITTLE BO-PEEP.
THE MARRIAGE OF THE THREE
LITTLE KITTENS. X
PUSSIE'S PARTY.
LITTLE TOM TUCKER
JACK SPRAT.

Colored.
* Same Books without the Music.

AUNT EFFIE'S.

HISTORY OF AN APPLE PIE.
ALADDIN ; or, WONDERFUL LAMP.
LITTLE DAME CRUMP.
CINDERELLA, OR GLASS SLIPPER.
LITTLE RED RIDING HOOD.
THE CHILDREN I. THE WOOD.

Aunt Oddamadodds Series.

LITTLE MISS CONSEQUENCE.
STORY OF THE SPOILT FROCK.
NAUGHTY BOYS.
NAUGHTY GIRLS.
LITTLE HEADS & LITTLE HEARTS.
FUNNY PHYSIC, FUNNY PICTURES.
COMIC CRUMBS.
COMICAL PICTURES.
FUNNY PICTURES, FOOD, &c.
ONE, TWO, BUCKLE MY SHOE.
SILVER SIXPENCE.
FOOLISH BOYS AND GIRLS.

Colored.

Dame Wonders.

THE LITTLE DRUMMER.
THE LITTLE TRAVELER.
THE LITTLE SAILOR BOY
ANIMALS AND BIRDS.
MISS ROSE.
MASTER ROSE.
MARY GOODCHILD.
HOW GEO. WORTHY Became MAYOR.
AMUSING ALPHABET.
MULTIPLICATION TABLE.
TABLE BOOK.

Colored.

MRS. ELLIOT'S STORIES.

BEAUTY BUT SKIN DEEP
THE LITTLE MIMIC.
THE LOST CHICKEN.
THE GREEDY CHILD CURED.
THE CONTRAST ; or, HOW TO BE
HAPPY.
THE BIRD'S NEST.

Colored.

Cinderella Series.

CINDERELLA.
TOM THUMB.
BABES IN THE WOOD.
THE THREE YOUNG CROWS.
HOUSE THAT JACK BUILT
ALPHABET & FUNNY PICTURES

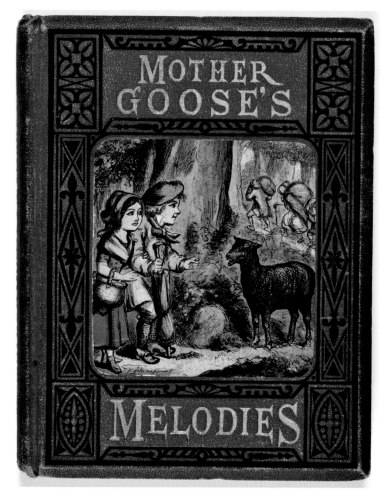

Cat. 38. *Mother Goose's Melodies*, 1878.

36. **D. A. G. "Baa Baa Black Sheep, Have You Any Wool?" Pen and ink with watercolor for MOTHER GOOSE, ca. 1870.**

37. **Unknown artist. "Pied Piper Playing for the Children." Pen and ink with watercolor for MOTHER GOOSE, ca. 1870.**
    Image, cover.

38. **MOTHER GOOSE'S MELODIES. New York: McLoughlin Brothers, 1878.**
    Gift of Herbert H. Hosmer, 1978.

From its earliest days until the twentieth century, McLoughlin Brothers published many editions of the traditional rhymes of *Mother Goose*, often reusing artwork from edition to edition. The original watercolors for *Mother Goose* were kept on file and were in constant use by the firm. The small watercolor by an unidentified artist (known by the initials D. A. G.) was used to illustrate "Baa Baa Black Sheep." It appeared inside a circa 1870 edition full of familiar childhood rhymes and was also later reused on the cover of *Mother Goose's Melodies*, published in 1878. The watercolor composition of the Pied Piper was copied from a competitor and was in use by McLoughlin Brothers repeatedly between 1870 and 1880.

39. Thomas Cuzner, engraver. ONE TWO BUCKLE MY SHOE. Aunt Oddamadodd Series. New York: McLoughlin Brothers, 1859–1862.

40. CINDERELLA. Fairy Moonbeam Series. New York: McLoughlin Brothers, 1876.
   Gift of Herbert H. Hosmer, 1978.

41. COCK ROBIN. Big Picture Books for Little Children. New York: McLoughlin Brothers, ca. 1865.
   Gift of Herbert H. Hosmer, 1978.

One reason for the success of McLoughlin Brothers was its early adaptation and commitment to issuing books in series, such as the Aunt Oddamadodd, Fairy Moonbeam, and Big Picture Books series. Retelling stories, reusing illustrations, and repurposing designs in multiple formats allowed the company to maximize revenue, from one-penny books (cats. 42, 44) to full-sized picture books like *Cock Robin*, which sold for thirty-seven cents.

42. THE NOISY BOY. Young America Series. New York: McLoughlin Brothers, ca. 1867.
   Gift of Diana and Colin Brown, 1994.

43. Printing block for NOISY BOY, ca. 1867.
   Gift of Herbert H. Hosmer, 1978.
   Image, p. 42.

44. DISORDERLY GIRL. Young America Series. Electrotyped by Vincent Dill. New York: McLoughlin Brothers, ca. 1867.
   Gift of Herbert H. Hosmer, 1978.
   Image, p. 14.

These very modest printings were marketed at the lowest end of the McLoughlin Brothers' catalog, retailing at one cent per copy. The books sold to retailers at one dollar for a gross (144 copies), so the profit on their sale was attractive to resellers. The Young America Series was issued in 1866 and 1867 and featured six moralistic titles about poorly behaved and well-behaved children, each illustrated with black-and-white images.

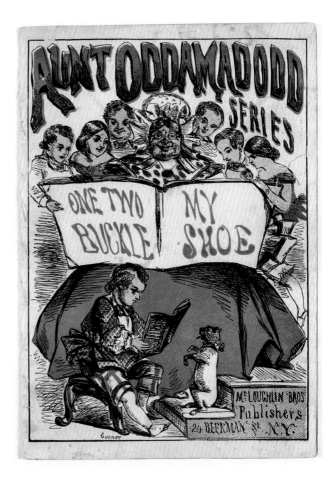

Cat. 39. *One Two Buckle My Shoe,* ca. 1859.

The only color was a single red block, used on the cover. The original woodblock for the black portion of the cover of *Noisy Boy* is part of the archive of McLoughlin Brothers material housed at the American Antiquarian Society. This block likely served as a master matrix and was reproduced as a durable electrotyped plate for printing. Vincent Dill, the electrotyper listed on other titles in the series, shared an address with McLoughlin Brothers from 1859 to 1866.

45. PICTURE ALPHABET. Illustrations by Justin Howard. New York: McLoughlin Brothers, 1861–1870.

Gift of Herbert H. Hosmer, 1978.

Image, pp. 66-67.

While issuing books as part of a series was a marketing strategy employed by many booksellers, McLoughlin Brothers took the practice to a new level. The back cover of *Picture Alphabet*, published by McLoughlin Brothers in the 1860s, gives a good sense of the firm's early production. Most impressive is the sheer number of series titles offered. Fifteen different series are listed, encompassing nearly 150 titles, all sold in both colored and plain versions. Mother Goose has her own section, as do primers and games. McLoughlin Brothers continued to list available titles and new products on the back covers of its books into the 1890s. This allowed consumers to have ready reference to McLoughlin Brothers stock, enabling them to easily find more titles similar to the one in hand.

46. TOM TEARABOUT. Father's Series. New York: McLoughlin Brothers, 1867.

Gift of Herbert H. Hosmer, 1978.

47. MY MOTHER. Mother's Series. New York: McLoughlin Brothers, 1867.

Gift of Herbert H. Hosmer, 1978.

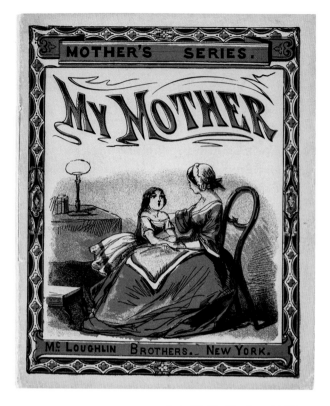

Cat. 47. *My Mother,* **1867.**

Although the number of series listed on the back of *Picture Alphabet* (cat. 45) is impressive, McLoughlin Brothers had even more for sale than what appeared on such lists and was constantly adding titles. In 1867 the firm introduced six new books each in the Mother's and Father's series, including *My Mother* and *Tom Tearabout*. These titles with colored covers were marketed by the company as "toy books" and sold retail at six cents each, wholesale at $4.50 for 144 copies. The company cleverly interspersed old favorites, like *Puss in Boots* and *Valentine & Orson*, in most new series, along with fresh, intriguingly titled books such as *The Butterfly's Ball* and *Miss Vanity's Holiday*.

48. THIS IS THE HOUSE THAT JACK BUILT. Pleasure Books Series. New York: McLoughlin Brothers, ca. 1865.

49. Publisher's mock up based on John Absolon and Harrison Weir, engravers. THE HOUSE THAT JACK BUILT. New York: Elton & Co., ca. 1851.

Unlike the Big Picture (cat. 41) and Aunt Oddamadodd (cat. 39) series, the Pleasure Books Series was intended to serve the lower end of the children's book market. Books like *This Is the House That Jack Built* sold for just six cents each and were positioned as budget printings of old favorites. Even at that low price, several of the sixteen interior illustrations were printed in full color. The book is paired here with a mock up from the McLoughlin Brothers archive that used a

cut-up earlier edition of the story published by Elton & Company. The Elton & Company edition did not offer any color illustrations and paired one page of text with one illustration. McLoughlin Brothers increased the size of the images, added color, and illustrated both sides of a spread, making the book more visually appealing.

50. LITTLE JACOB, AND HOW HE BECAME FAT. Little Slovenly Peter Series. New York: McLoughlin Brothers, 1866.

Gift of Herbert H. Hosmer, 1978.

McLoughlin Brothers rarely missed an opportunity to create books for new audiences. In 1866 it started to issue "indestructible" books, printed on linen. These titles were intended for the youngest children whose toddler enthusiasm could damage paper-bound picture books. The method of printing in color on tear-resistant fabric was copied by McLoughlin Brothers from companies in England who had been issuing titles in cloth since 1860. This title was one of a series of six, all "printed in oil" on linen and offered wholesale for $4.50 per gross (144 copies). McLoughlin's 1867 catalog lists twenty-two titles on linen. The format must have been popular as the brothers continued to expand their linen book line into the 1890s. The 1899 season trade catalog lists over one hundred titles available on linen, which are touted as "best adapted to the smaller children."

Cat. 51. *Game of Visit to Camp*, ca. 1863.

Cat. 54. "Topsy," from *Eva St. Claire and Topsey*, 1870.

51. GAME OF VISIT TO CAMP. New York: McLoughlin Brothers, ca. 1863.

52. MINTY GREEN. Series 2. New York: McLoughlin Brothers, ca. 1865.

53. Edward P. Cogger, engraver. **GENERAL TOM THUMB.** Series 3. New York: McLoughlin Brothers, ca. 1865.

54. Edward P. Cogger, engraver. **EVA ST. CLAIRE AND TOPSEY.** New York: McLoughlin Brothers, 1870.
Gift of Herbert H. Hosmer, 1984.

Like their father and Robert H. Elton before them, the McLoughlin brothers included games and paper toys in their stock from the beginning of the firm in 1858.

One of their earliest games was a Civil War–themed card game, *Visit to Camp*, where each player chose a character from a colonel to a vivandière (canteen keeper). The associated cards for that character (including weapons, tools, and clothing) were then gathered through a series of exchanges among the players. This game was on offer until about 1870.

McLoughlin Brothers produced an extensive line of paper dolls, starting with tiny one-cent dolls (Series 1: a doll and two outfits) and up to twenty-cent dolls (Series 4: two dolls and fancier, multipart outfits). *Minty Green* was a Series 2 doll and sold for ten cents. Paper dolls of all kinds, from uniformed paper soldiers (cat. 191) to brides, would remain a part of the company's production until after 1940.

The firm also often capitalized on current events to promote its books and games. McLoughlin Brothers produced a paper doll of Charles Sherwood Stratton (1838–1883), better known as Tom Thumb, during the height of the performer's fame. This set sold for fifteen cents retail and included many of the costumes worn by Stratton during his performances with P. T. Barnum. The firm also published dolls of Eva St. Clair and Topsy based on Harriet Beecher Stowe's *Uncle Tom's Cabin*, one of the most widely read books in the country. This set (also offered in a penny version) continued to be listed in the company's catalogs until 1879.

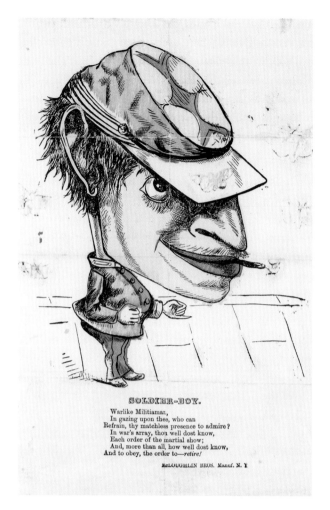 

Cats. 55 & 56. *Soldier-Boy,* ca. 1865, and *Thine For Ever,* ca. 1870.

55. SOLDIER-BOY. Comic valentine. New York: McLoughlin Brothers, ca. 1865.

56. THINE FOR EVER. Sentimental valentine. New York: McLoughlin Brothers, ca. 1870.

John McLoughlin Jr. learned about the production of valentines when he served as an apprentice. The craze for sentimental and comic valentines peaked during the Civil War years in America and continued until the end of the century. Although outside the realm of children's publishing, there was profit to be had and so McLoughlin Brothers issued valentines annually. The firm's catalog for 1875 stated, "[W]e have no hesitation in asserting the superiority of our Valentines over those heretofore placed before the public. Our large experience and increasing facilities place within our reach the finest materials and most skillful artists and workmen. . . . A large amount of the material used by us is manufactured upon our own premises. This enables us to furnish a superior quality of Valentines at low prices." Each year the brothers added more and more designs. In 1879, they offered one hundred new comic valentines, declaring in their catalog that "these contain racy, pungent hits, very cleverly executed, and apply to every phase of the human character, and are, we believe, better than any that have ever before been produced."

57. Children's Favorite, Animals & Birds. The Favorite Series. Illustrated by Justin H. Howard. Plate house copy. New York: McLoughlin Brothers, 1866.

Gift of Herbert Hosmer, 1978.

First published in 1866, this copy of *Children's Favorite, Animals & Birds* was retained as a plate house copy by McLoughlin Brothers and was filed in its archives for reference. The book was one of six titles in the Favorite Series, which retailed at thirty-seven cents each. The series was promoted as "beautiful picture books for the young, printed in oil colors" issued on "stiff board covers." This series was one of the earliest where McLoughlin highlighted the illustrator, artist Justin H. Howard (fl. 1856–1880), who created the images for each title in the series. In the future, McLoughlin would more actively engage and promote American illustrators in the development of its picture book line.

58. Mrs. Grive. Creation of the World and the Deluge. Half Hours with the Bible Series. Illustrations by H. W. Herrick. Stereotyped by Vincent Dill. New York: McLoughlin Brothers, 1867.

In the 1860s, McLoughlin Brothers launched a successful series of books of stories drawn from the Bible, including this one which retells tales from the Book of Genesis. As the majority of McLoughlin's customer base practiced the Christian faith, these titles were steady sellers. These books were issued for fifteen cents each with plain illustrations or twenty-five cents each with colored plates. Eventually there were twelve titles in all. The firm pirated the text for all twelve titles

from an 1862 series issued in London by Ward & Lock.[8] They even swiped the promotional copy that appeared on the back of the book: "This entirely new series of beautifully illustrated Bible stories for the Young has been prepared with extreme care so as to render them easy to be understood by the Infant mind." In its 1867 catalog, McLoughlin Brothers stated that the series was "Elegantly illustrated by H. W. Herrick," one of the artists who was part of the firm's productive stable of illustrators. Naming Herrick marked a change for the firm, and promoting artists would become one of its trademark marketing methods in the decades to come.

ILLUSTRATORS AT MCLOUGHLIN BROTHERS

For decades, McLoughlin Brothers maintained a large stable of artists, using their varied and distinct talents to illustrate hundreds of picture books. According to the company's history, seventy-five artists were employed at the firm's Brooklyn factory from 1870 to about 1915. Some artists appear to have been retained as staff, and others worked freelance. In the earliest days of the firm, McLoughlin Brothers rarely identified the individuals who created the images inside its books, giving no credit on the covers or title pages of its products. Some engravers cannily included their names in their wood-engraved blocks (cats. 53, 54), but before about 1865, the names of the artists who designed the illustrations were usually unknown.

Around the time of the American Civil War, McLoughlin Brothers began to print the names of a few illustrators on the covers of its books. Men like Justin H. Howard (fl. 1856–1890) and Thomas Nast (1840–1902) had already gained reputations for their visual contributions to both comic periodicals and the illustrated press and would have been known to a broad segment of American society. Brandishing the names of artists like Nast, who was extremely well known in his lifetime, added caché to McLoughlin Brothers books for children. The relationship must have been beneficial for both parties, as Howard and Nast both had multiyear relationships with McLoughlin Brothers. Eventually, many women would be employed as illustrators by the firm as well, and several of these, including Sarah Noble Ives (1864–1944) and Ida Waugh (1846–1919), would be credited for their contributions.

The staff artists at McLoughlin Brothers were kept busy producing creative and innovative illustrations for a wide variety of publications, from *Mother Goose* to books with patriotic themes. They also did a lot of copy work. McLoughlin Brothers, like many book publishers of the day, copied hundreds of titles by others and reissued them under its own imprint, usually undercutting its competition in the process. The portion of the firm's art archive preserved at the American Antiquarian Society holds over 1,500 examples of watercolors and drawings including exact copies of works by other illustrators and original sketches. Considered within the larger scope of the firm's published output, this collection offers a unique perspective on the bookmaking practices of the company. Some of the drawings appear not to have been used. Were the unpublished watercolors and drawings retained for future projects? Does the high number of drawings of Santa Claus and biblical scenes indicate that these topics were constantly revisited for book production ideas? Although the answers to these questions may never be known with certainty, the fact that the illustrations themselves were carefully filed and preserved indicates that they were considered to be a valuable asset by the McLoughlin brothers.

Cat. 61. *The Great Serpent and His Tricks*, 1881.

59. THE CATS' PARTY. Dame Dingle's Series. New York: McLoughlin Brothers, 1869.

Gift of Herbert H. Hosmer, 1978.

Image, cover.

60. Justin H. Howard. "The Dance," from THE CATS' PARTY. Watercolor, gouache, pen and ink, ca. 1869.

Gift of Herbert H. Hosmer, 1978.

61. William Bruton. "The Great Serpent and His Tricks." Unpublished illustrator's mock up, 1881.

Image, pp. 76-77.

The illustrations for *The Cats' Party* were made by American artist Justin H. Howard and ably capture the high spirits and energy of the tale. Howard started his career in 1856 drawing for comic papers like *Yankee Notions*. He started working for the McLoughlin brothers in about 1860. His original watercolor of a dancing scene, which includes corrections and color changes, is part of the firm's art archive and provides valuable evidence of the production process at McLoughlin Brothers. Most corrections made on the original art are reflected in the printed version.

The illustrator's mock up for "The Great Serpent" was made by one of the firm's staff artists, William Bruton (ca. 1855–1885), who began creating images for McLoughlin Brothers in the 1870s. The graphite sketches show an enormous snake who is used as a fire hose, a tightrope, and an anchor. Bruton also produced a similar mock up for a tale entitled "King Pin," which is also preserved at AAS. Neither tale seems to have been published by McLoughlin Brothers.

62. THE FAT BOY, FROM DICKENS' PICKWICK. Illustrations by Thomas Nast. New York: McLoughlin Brothers, 1882.

Thomas Nast began his association with McLoughlin Brothers in the 1860s after working as a successful cartoonist for *Frank Leslie's Illustrated Newspaper* and

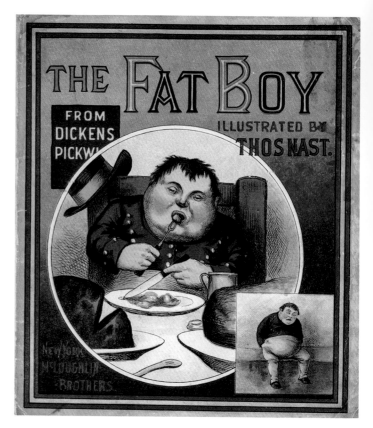

Cat. 62. *The Fat Boy*, 1882.

Harper's Weekly. During the Civil War, Nast became a household name in America and was thanked by President Lincoln for encouraging enlistment in the Union Army. He is the artist most people associate with McLoughlin Brothers because of a series of books featuring Santa Claus that he produced in the 1860s and 1870s (cats. 152, 155). In fact, Nast completed less than a dozen titles for McLoughlin, but he always had his name featured prominently on the cover, as seen on this chromolithographed edition of *The Fat Boy*. This lesser-known Nast-McLoughlin publication is a rhyming version of a tale extracted from Charles Dickens's *The Pickwick Papers*.

63. Henry W. Herrick. **Cover design for New, Childs First Book. Watercolor, pen and ink, ca. 1897.**

64. Heinrich Hoffman. **Pauline and the Matches.** Aunt Lulu's Series. New York: McLoughlin Brothers, ca. 1867.
Gift of Herbert H. Hosmer, 1978.

65. "Poverty Town," in **Aunt Louisa's Golden Gift.** New York: McLoughlin Brothers, ca. 1879.
Gift of Herbert H. Hosmer, 1978.

Henry W. Herrick (1824–1906) was a prolific illustrator and art instructor, creating images for *Harper's Weekly* and *Appleton's*, as well as book illustrations for Hurd & Houghton, Louis Prang & Company, and McLoughlin Brothers. He taught at the New York School of Design for Women and at Yale College. After 1865 he turned to watercolor painting, exhibiting his work at the National Academy of Design. His watercolor of a contented cat is part of the McLoughlin Brothers art archive. It started as a book cover in 1897 but was later reused as an inside illustration in *Our Four-Footed Friends*, published in 1900.

Herrick was skilled at human figure work and he was one of the artists, along with Thomas Nast and Justin H. Howard, to be regularly credited by McLoughlin Brothers on the cover or title pages of their books. His designs appear in a wide range of titles, from *Pauline and the Matches* (twelve cents wholesale, twenty-five cents retail) to a fancy bound edition of *Aunt Louisa's Golden Gift*, which included a compilation of over twenty short stories and verses paired with elegant, bronze-tinted illustrations and sold for $1.50 in bookshops.

Cat. 65. "Poverty Town,"
Aunt Louisa's Golden Gift,
ca. 1879.

66. Paul Pryor. THE LIFE OF GENERAL PUTNAM. Illustrated by Justin H. Howard. New York: McLoughlin Brothers, 1879–1885.

Gift of Herbert H. Hosmer, 1978.

67. A PEEP AT BUFFALO BILL'S WILD WEST. New York: McLoughlin Brothers, 1887.

Gift of Herbert H. Hosmer, 1978.

Image, p. 145.

68. Justin H. Howard. "And the Squaws and Papooses Ride on Ahead," from A PEEP AT BUFFALO BILL'S WILD WEST. Watercolor, pen & ink, ca. 1887.

Gift of Herbert H. Hosmer, 1978.

Justin H. Howard was an experienced cartoonist and illustrator who produced pictures for dozens of McLoughlin Brothers titles. He produced original work for several books with American topics, including a biography of General Israel Putnam and a picture book relating the adventures of Buffalo Bill Cody, an American performer who started his famous Wild West shows in 1883. McLoughlin Brothers' timing for the 1887 release of the latter could not have been better—in May of 1887, Cody and his troupe performed for Queen Victoria in London, an event widely covered in the press.

Howard's images always included action and often leaned towards the humorous (cat. 94), but he was also skilled at capturing more serious emotions. His watercolor of Native Americans on the move is a poignant reminder that western expansion displaced families. The text reads: "And driven away by the white man's axe / From the early haunts of his race / The Indian packs his tents and makes tracks / For a suitable dwelling place. . . . This is the game of hide and seek / That white men and red men play / On the prairies wide, where on every side / They fight for the right of way." Howard's colorful image was reduced to a three-color lithograph on the press, an editorial decision that gave more visual weight to an image of settlers in a covered wagon that appeared on the opposing page.

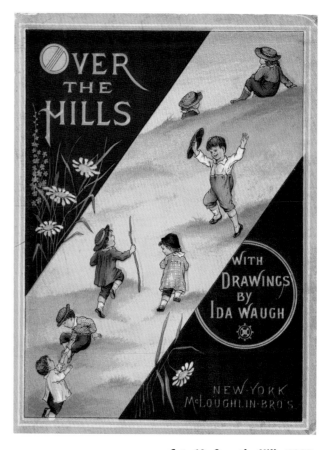

Cat. 69. *Over the Hills***, 1882.**

69. OVER THE HILLS, A COLLECTION OF JUVENILE PICTURES IN COLORS BY MISS IDA WAUGH. New York: McLoughlin Brothers, 1882.

Gift of Herbert H. Hosmer, 1978.

Because of the overwhelming popularity of English picture books featuring dainty children in antique dress drawn by English illustrator Kate Greenaway (1846–1901), McLoughlin Brothers hired American artist Ida Waugh to create illustrations in a similar style. Waugh produced seven titles in 1882 for McLoughlin Brothers and later worked for its Boston competitors, E. P. Dutton & Company and Louis Prang & Company. She had studied art at the Académie Julien and the Académie Delecluse in Paris, as well as at the Pennsylvania Academy of Fine Arts. Waugh worked successfully as a

**Cat. 68. Howard, "And the Squaws and
Papooses Ride on Ahead," ca. 1887.**

sculptor and a painter, often winning prizes and critical acclaim for her work. Starting in 1883, following her success with McLoughlin, Waugh began illustrating verses written by Amy Blanchard, her long-time partner.

70. CINDERELLA. Illustrations by Richard André. New York: McLoughlin Brothers, ca. 1888.

Gift of Herbert H. Hosmer, 1978.

British artist Richard André (born William Roger Snow (1834–1907)) first worked with McLoughlin Brothers to illustrate the children's travel picture book *By Land & Water* in 1887. It is quite probable that out of this relationship came several illustrated fairy tales for McLoughlin, including this version of *Cinderella*. André's art-nouveau-style cover illustration is not only a fine example of color printing in which the colors are blended to produce a wide palette of shades, it is also a sophisticated visual montage that incorporates several elements of the Cinderella story in a single design, with its dreamy Cinderella at the fireside framed by the lizard and rats crawling around a pumpkin, anticipating their magical transformations.

71. OLD KING COLE. Mother Goose Melodies Series. New York: McLoughlin Brothers, 1888.

72. Chester Loomis. "Mother Goose." Watercolor, pen & ink, ca. 1900.

Gift of Herbert H. Hosmer, 1978.

Mother Goose was a steady seller for McLoughlin Brothers, and the firm would rely on multiple illustrators over the years to give the Mother Goose rhymes a fresh look. In 1888, it used humorous illustrations by Charles Kendrick (1841–1914) for a sixteen-page linen book of nursery rhymes intended for small hands. Kendrick worked for *Frank Leslie's Illustrated Weekly* in the 1870s and 1880s and was called "one of the best of our rising young artists" by *Century*

Magazine in 1881. This copy of Old King Cole is a plate house copy and was retained by the firm for reference, which explains the excellent condition and the editorial annotations.

Over a decade later, McLoughlin Brothers hired Chester Loomis (1852–1924), a respected landscape and portrait painter who was trained at the Académie Julian in Paris, to produce illustrations for a potential Mother Goose reissue. Loomis used the pseudonym "Valnotte" on this watercolor of a kindly looking Mother Goose. Several other watercolors in the McLoughlin Brothers archive and two published titles in the Society's book collection bear this signature, indicating that Loomis took on regular commissions for the firm between 1900 and 1907.

Cat. 72. Loomis, "Mother Goose," ca. 1900.

73. Georgina A. Davis. "Rumpelstiltskin." Watercolor, gouache, ca. 1885.

Gift of Herbert H. Hosmer, 1978.

Georgina A. Davis (ca. 1852–1901) was trained at the Cooper Union Female School of Design, exhibited paintings and etchings in Boston and New York, and supported herself for over thirty years as a commercial illustrator. During the decades between 1880 and 1900 when she submitted illustrations to McLoughlin Brothers, she also produced over a hundred images for *Frank Leslie's Illustrated Newspaper*, where she worked as a staff artist and reporter.[9] McLoughlin hired many women illustrators, and Davis, perhaps because her work at *Leslie's* had put her name before the public, was often credited by the firm.

This large watercolor of the miller's daughter explaining her plight to Rumpelstiltskin is part of the company's art archives, along with watercolors of Snow White, Red Riding Hood, and images of children with pets and toys, all done by Davis. Several of these were published by the brothers in the 1890s, although a printed version of Rumpelstiltskin with this illustration has not been located. All are expertly painted and reflect the skill and many years of education and experience that made Davis a success.

Cat. 74. Grosvenor, cover design for *The Three Bears*, ca. 1900.

74. Attr. to Fredrika Grosvenor. Cover design for THE THREE BEARS. Watercolor, pen and ink, ca. 1900.

Gift of Herbert H. Hosmer, 1978.

This design for an unpublished edition of *The Three Bears* is attributed to the California artist Fredrika Grosvenor, who wrote and illustrated two other titles for the McLoughlin firm. Often the existence in the McLoughlin archives of an object like this watercolor leads to more questions than answers. Was the market oversaturated with versions of the fairy tale? Did this design lead the company to support Grosvenor's 1905 title, *A Very Small Tale of Two Very Small Bears*? Like the mock up for "The Great Serpent and his Tricks" (cat. 61) and the watercolor from *Rumpelstiltskin* (cat. 73), this unpublished drawing offers important insight into the editorial actions, business decisions, and production operations of McLoughlin Brothers.

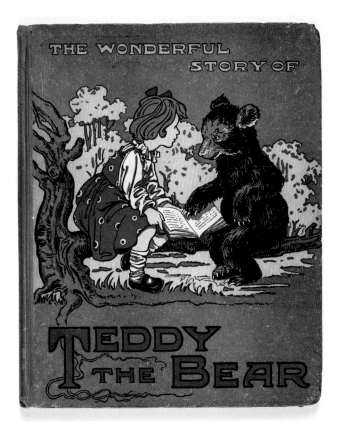

Cat. 75. *The Story of Teddy the Bear,* **ca. 1907.**

75. Sarah Noble Ives. THE STORY OF TEDDY THE BEAR. New York: McLoughlin Brothers, ca. 1907.

Gift of Herbert H. Hosmer, 1978.

76. Sarah Noble Ives. "Mother! Oh, If She Were Only Here," from THE STORY OF TEDDY THE BEAR. Watercolor, pen and ink, graphite, with paste-over, ca. 1907.

Written and illustrated by artist Sarah Noble Ives, this book tells the story of a little bear cub separated from its mother. By naming her protagonist "Teddy," Ives gave a nod to President Theodore Roosevelt and a famous 1902 incident in which he spared the life of a captive bear. The book sold for seventy-five cents and it went through three editions before 1932. Ives not only wrote the text for *Teddy the Bear*, she also provided six watercolor illustrations. She used foliage to frame each design, creating a stained-glass effect that looked fresh and modern in McLoughlin Brothers' line. Part of the firm's archive, this watercolor is annotated with color notes by the press team and has a paste-over correcting the caption lettering. Ives grew up near Detroit, Michigan, and studied art in New York and Paris. She kept a studio in New York and later in Boston before moving to California in 1924. Her work for McLoughlin includes approximately fifteen titles published between 1885 and 1920.

77. Sarah Noble Ives. Four watercolors from CINDERELLA. Watercolor, gouache, pen and ink, ca. 1912.

Sarah Noble Ives, who worked for McLoughlin Brothers on multiple projects (cats. 75, 76), was among the first generation of women artists to become prominent picture book illustrators. Like other women working in a male-dominated occupation, Ives did not always use her first name. She frequently signed her work, as she did on these images for *Cinderella*, "Noble Ives" to mask her gender. In these watercolors, Ives portrays Cinderella as a pre-Raphaelite beauty who commands center stage. The illustrations are very different from images in earlier editions of the fairy tale published by McLoughlin Brothers. With their sinuous lines reflecting the stylistic influences of art nouveau, Ives's paintings convey a more sophisticated Cinderella for a new generation of twentieth-century picture book consumers.

78. Frances Bassett Comstock. Binding design for Tanglewood Tales. Pen and ink, ca. 1910.

79. Nathaniel Hawthorne. Tanglewood Tales. New York: McLoughlin Brothers, 1910.

A good publisher's binding is eye-catching and causes a potential buyer to pick up the volume and, perhaps, purchase it as well. This 1910 book was described in the McLoughlin Brothers' catalog as "a very handsome edition of Hawthorne's admirable version of the ancient Greek mythological fables." The original pen and ink submission for the binding design for *Tanglewood Tales* was made by artist Frances Bassett Comstock (1881–1922). It is housed in the Society's McLoughlin Brothers art archive with twenty images of kings, centaurs, a minotaur, and witches by Comstock, which were all used to illustrate the volume.

Comstock was born in Ohio and studied art with Frederick W. Freer at the Art Institute in Chicago. In 1905 she married Enos Comstock, also an artist, and the couple settled in New Jersey. Both worked at McLoughlin Brothers as staff artists in the early part of the twentieth century and made the transition with the firm to Springfield, Massachusetts, after its purchase by Milton Bradley in 1920. Frances also worked for Houghton Mifflin and Rand McNally & Company and exhibited her work at the New York Watercolor Club. Her drawing style is confident and direct, and her work with the human figure was described by one publisher as "whimsical, fanciful and fantastic."[10]

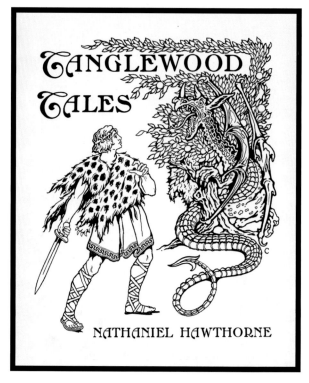

Cat. 78. *Tanglewood Tales,* **ca. 1910, above.**

Cat. 77. Ives, "At the Ball," ca. 1912, opposite page.

DIFFICULTIES OF NINETEENTH-CENTURY HUMOR

Children's books have historically played a role in introducing children to cultural norms, using words and pictures to reinforce moral messages and encourage appropriate behavior. This is particularly true in humorous tales where a protagonist's pratfalls were designed to empower children to point out right and wrong. While many McLoughlin Brothers books contain silly rhymes or are full of ridiculous incongruities that make children laugh, other titles in this genre can be viewed today as representative of a society desperately attempting to maintain its status quo.

Looking closely at many McLoughlin Brothers titles offers perceptive modern viewers a glimpse of some of the difficult issues of America's Gilded Age (1880–1900), a time of great social and political disorder. Thousands of European and Asian immigrants were pouring into cities along the coasts, and Native people were being forcibly displaced across the West. Recently emancipated slaves were driven into sharecropping or moved away from the South seeking opportunities. Large swathes of political power were being consolidated by members of corrupt organizations like Tammany Hall and women rallied against the establishment for the right to vote.

Many of McLoughlin's primarily white, lower- and middle-class customers were surrounded by the social upheaval that resulted from these events. They sought out books and games for their children that poked fun at people not like them, reducing them to caricatures and stereotypes. The demeaning of the "other," the "not-like-us" exclusionary tone, and the violent actions masquerading as an amusing part of childhood innocence, were all acceptable narratives.

Comic titles that dealt with race, gender, and ethnicity were among the most popular books in McLoughlin Brothers' catalogs. Many books, including *Ten Little Niggers*, remained steady sellers for the firm for decades. These books are reminders of a past from which we have become, by the authority of time and events, very nearly disconnected, and yet they also echo many of the challenges, from inequality to violence, that American society faces today.

Cat. 85. *Brownie Year Book*, 1895.

80. **JINGLES & JOKES FOR LITTLE FOLKS. Joyful Tales Series. New York: McLoughlin Brothers, 1869.**

Gift of Herbert H. Hosmer, 1978.

81. **JINGLES AND JOKES FOR LITTLE FOLKS. Punch & Judy Series. New York: McLoughlin Brothers, 1903.**

Gift of Herbert H. Hosmer, 1978.

These two joke books, issued over thirty years apart, are remarkably similar in their content. Different amusing and moralistic rhymes are bound together in colorful paper covers. The earlier edition includes simple two-color illustrations, while the later features chromolithographed pictures on each page. The books do not include one-liner jokes as we understand them today—the rhymes are more like multipart limericks. For example: "Wicked Willie Wimble / Stole his Granny's thimble / And she could not catch him / Because she was not nimble." While some old chestnuts are included, like Peter, Peter, Pumpkin Eater, the majority, including one about a sailor in a tiny boat who chants, "I've come from a land from over the seas / Where oysters grow on apple trees," have been forgotten by today's readers.

Cat. 81. *Jingles and Jokes for Little Folks,* **1903.**

82. **"Three Wise Men from Gotham." In MOTHER GOOSE IN A NEW DRESS. Illustrations by Walter Satterlee. New York: McLoughlin Brothers, 1882.**

Gift of Herbert H. Hosmer, 1978.
Image, p. 4.

83. **SIMPLE SIMON. Little Dot Series. New York: McLoughlin Brothers, 1897.**

Gift of Herbert H. Hosmer, 1978.

Many of the traditional Mother Goose rhymes are full of incongruities that were intended to be silly (three wise men in a bowl?). Being good businessmen, the McLoughlin brothers consistently issued editions of *Mother Goose* during all the decades they were publishing. This deluxe volume of familiar rhymes features illustrations by Walter Satterlee (1844–1908),

an American painter based in Brooklyn best known for his figure studies and genre paintings. The linen "indestructible" edition of *Simple Simon* was made for the youngest children. Simon, who first appeared in an English chapbook in the 1760s, is mocked repeatedly, stanza after stanza, for melting a snowball by the fire, fishing in a bucket, and washing himself with shoe polish. His mental shortcomings could be pointed out by young readers and were likely laughed at by adults and children alike.

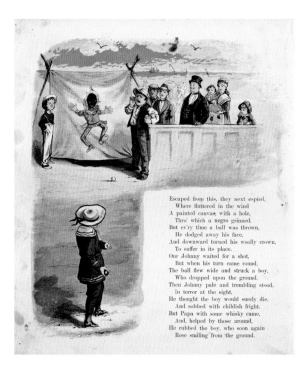

Cats. 86 & 87. *Johnny Headstrong's Trip to Coney Island,* 1882, and *Yankee Doodle,* ca. 1890.

84. Brownie's Nine Pins Bowling Game. New York: McLoughlin Brothers, 1890s.

Image, p. 9.

85. Palmer Cox. Brownie Year Book. New York: McLoughlin Brothers, 1895.

Image, pp. 88-89.

The figures on these bowling pins are based on small, multi-ethnic, fairy-like characters invented and drawn by Canadian artist and author Palmer Cox (1840–1924). In 1881, the "brownies" appeared in poems and stories that circulated in illustrated periodicals across the United States. The adventures of these mischievous little men of all nationalities quickly became an international phenomenon. Cox's brownies appeared in dozens of books for children from 1879 to 1924, published by a variety of firms, including D. Appleton & Company, Century Company, and McLoughlin Brothers. They also appeared on dishes, fabric, and toys (like these pins), and Kodak even named a camera after them. Many

historians consider the sprites to be the first example of mass-marketing using cartoon figures. Their antics were definitely humorous and would have appealed to children of all ages.

86. Johnny Headstrong's Trip to Coney Island. Illustrated by William Bruton. New York: McLoughlin Brothers, 1882.

Gift of Herbert H. Hosmer, 1978.

87. Yankee Doodle. Illustrated by Thomas Nast. New York: McLoughlin Brothers, ca. 1890.

Gift of Herbert H. Hosmer, 1978.

Humor is an unpredictable characteristic. What makes one child laugh may be completely missed by another. But McLoughlin Brothers had several books that were successful and sold well, indicating that many children (or their parents) enjoyed them and were likely amused by them. One of these was *Johnny Headstrong's Trip to Coney Island*, which follows the story of a heedless boy on a family trip to the beach. The book received favorable press mentions in New York and London when it was released in the fall of 1882.[11] In the tale, Johnny falls into the ocean, rides a runaway donkey, and participates in an arcade game where the object was to throw a ball at an African American boy's face (he misses and hits a white bystander).

Another best seller was *Yankee Doodle*, which was first issued by McLoughlin Brothers around 1871. This circa 1890 edition is filled with humorous illustrations by American cartoonist and satirist Thomas Nast. Yankee Doodle has ridiculously long legs and wears brightly colored clothing. The volume includes many lesser-known verses to the popular tune, such as, "The people all went wild with joy / And set the bells to ringing / And some were eating ginger bread / And others loudly singing. . . . Yankee Doodle keep it up . . ."

88. **"The Girl Who Inked Herself and Her Book and How It Ended." In LITTLE MISS CONSEQUENCE. Aunt Oddamadodd Series. New York: McLoughlin Brothers, 1859–1862.**
Gift of Herbert H. Hosmer, 1978.

89. **Heinrich Hoffmann. INKY BOYS. Little Delights Series. New York: McLoughlin Brothers, 1875.**
Gift of Herbert H. Hosmer, 1978.

90. **LOTTIE AND DOTTIE, OR THE TWINS. Uncle Harry's Series. New York: McLoughlin Brothers, 1880.**

For decades, McLoughlin Brothers issued comic stories at all price points, from penny books up to deluxe chromolithographed editions. This trio exemplifies typical penny books marketed to the low end of the market, retailing for just three to five cents. These often contain cautionary tales focused on bad behavior. "The Girl Who Inked Herself," from about 1861, is the story of a white girl whose fascination with ink (she plays

Cat. 88. *Little Miss Consequence,* ca. 1859.

in it, sucks her pen, gets it on her clothes, and eventually spills it) changes her into a black mammy doll that her parents then sell to the rag man. *Inky Boys*, from 1875, relates the tale of a trio of boys who mock an African American man on the street. An angry Santa Claus punishes them by dipping them into a giant inkwell where they become permanently blackened. The story was one of a set of ten cautionary tales written in 1845 by a German psychiatrist. The Struwwelpeter stories, as they became known, gained immense popularity in America in the 1860s, and McLoughlin Brothers continued to issue editions at all price points well into the 1890s (cat. 171). These books reflect the unfortunate realities of

Cat. 92. *Life and Death of Rich Mrs. Duck,* 1882.

THE FUNERAL PROCESSION.

Quoth the lady, incensed at so rude a remark,
"I'm sure, Dr. Drake, you're treating my case quite in the
From anything that I eat it cannot possibly be,   [dark;
For I am careful, indeed, to an extraordinary degree!"
The fat lady's alarm, as thus she replied,
Was as much for her stomach as ~~also~~ her pride. *it was for*

both the pre–Civil War era, when issues of slavery were being widely debated, and of the Jim Crow era, which took hold in the United States in the 1870s. Racially charged content such as this is offensive to the modern reader but was considered humorous in the nineteenth century.

91. **Mr. Thomas Cat Bachelor. Granny Gooseberry Series. New York: McLoughlin Brothers, 1879–1889.**
Gift of Herbert H. Hosmer, 1978.

92. **Life and Death of Rich Mrs. Duck, a Notorious Glutton. Dame Dingle's Series. New York: McLoughlin Brothers, 1882.**
Gift of Herbert H. Hosmer, 1978.

Many comic titles in the McLoughlin Brothers canon will cause the modern reader to pause and ponder the complexities of humor in the nineteenth century. Anthropomorphized animals were frequently used in children's stories to emulate negative human character traits or poor behavior. Mr. Thomas Cat lives the life of a carefree bachelor, ignorant of how his escapades affect those around him. Eventually he marries and is so unhappy that he commits suicide by hanging. Mrs. Duck, whose overeating leads to ill health and eventually death from gluttony, is described as a "fat lady," adding a gendered layer to stereotypes around obesity. Both tales would have been perceived as highly comical in the 1880s. Today's reader is brought up short by these books. Under what circumstances could these events have been deemed funny or, perhaps more baffling, appropriate for children?

93. HISTORY OF PAT AND HIS QUEER LITTLE
    DOG. New York: Elton & Co., 1851.

94. Howard & Bisbee. LOOK BEFORE YOU LEAP,
    OR LEAP-YEAR LESSONS. Illustrations by
    Justin Howard. New York: McLoughlin
    Brothers, 1872.
    Gift of Herbert H. Hosmer, 1978.

95. Henry L. Stephens. FUN FROM THE FLOWERY
    LAND. New York: McLoughlin Brothers, ca.
    1882.
    Gift of Herbert H. Hosmer, 1978.

Cat. 95. *Fun from the*
Flowery Land, ca. 1882.

One consistent and unfortunate element of human
comedy is the tendency to use people unlike oneself
to serve as the butt of a joke. The "not like me" approach
was widely used by McLoughlin Brothers to sell comic
picture books for children. This method appears in a
book by Elton & Company, the precursor to McLoughlin
Brothers, which issued several anti-Irish titles,
including the 1851 *History of Pat and his Queer Little
Dog.* Between 1820 and 1860, 1.9 million immigrants
arrived in America to escape the Great Irish Famine.
Negative caricatures of Irish people quickly appeared in
political cartoons, print culture, and children's books,
as the nation struggled to adapt to perceived differences
between the immigrants and themselves. In 1872, just as
issues of women's suffrage were returning to the public
arena after the Civil War, McLoughlin Brothers issued
Look Before You Leap, a facetious story about unmarried
women who are made fun of on every page. The book
also reveals the era's intolerance of homosexuality by
indicating that certain "feminized" male sales clerks
were ineligible as partners, as only "men" were wanted.
Finally, in May of 1882, the Chinese Exclusion Act, the
first significant law restricting immigration to the United
States, was enacted. In the fall of that year, McLoughlin
released *Fun from the Flowery Land,* a picture book
full of negative stereotypes about Chinese people and
illustrated by images the firm called "amusing" but that
are now considered to be offensive.

Cat. 96. *The Merry Game of Old Maid,* **1898.**

96. THE MERRY GAME OF OLD MAID. New York: McLoughlin Brothers, 1898.

In western cultures, unmarried older women are often objects of humor, and many "old maids" appear in novels, theatrical performances, movies, and more. McLoughlin Brothers issued Old Maid games in many forms, the most common being card games. The game dates to the seventeenth century and involves pairing up cards until just one remains (the Old Maid). This 1898 board game takes a different approach, having the players assume the Old Maid persona as they move through the streets of the game, meeting all kinds of people in the neighborhood—some that slow them down (listening to a fish story told by a long-winded neighbor) and others that speed them up. Here the object is to avoid being the last Old Maid to make it to the center of the board. Numerous cultural and racial stereotypes fill the street, including "Count Dago" and "The Nigger." Today considered problematic, these terms were in common use in America during the nineteenth century.

97. TOPSY. Topsy Series. New York: McLoughlin Brothers, between 1894 and 1914.

98. TEN LITTLE NIGGERS. New York: McLoughlin Brothers, 1894.
Gift of Herbert H. Hosmer, 1978.

99. TEN LITTLE NIGGERS. Plate house copy. New York: McLoughlin Brothers, 1897.

McLoughlin Brothers produced numerous picture books for children that featured African Americans. None would be considered appropriate or humorous today. This shaped book capitalizes on the public's knowledge of Harriet Beecher Stowe's character Topsy from *Uncle Tom's Cabin, or Life Among the Lowly,* who graces the cover. Topsy was considered a wicked and uncontrolled comic character. However, the contents of this book have no relation at all to *Uncle Tom's Cabin.* Instead the pages are full of rhymes and images of African American children that are intended to be amusing, but by modern standards are full of negative racial stereotypes.

McLoughlin Brothers issued its first edition of *Ten Little Niggers* around 1872. The extremely violent verses where individuals are killed off one by one until only one remains, are based on a blackface minstrel song of the same title first performed in 1869. Minstrel shows, where white performers sang and danced in black face, were popular around the world during the last quarter of the nineteenth century. These volumes are, in a sense, minstrel shows in miniature. As historian Elizabeth Pryor of Smith College has said, "Jim Crow dances off the stage and into the home" through these picture books.[12] Clearly intended for a white audience, the books were intended as amusement but they subversively indoctrinated children in white paternalism.

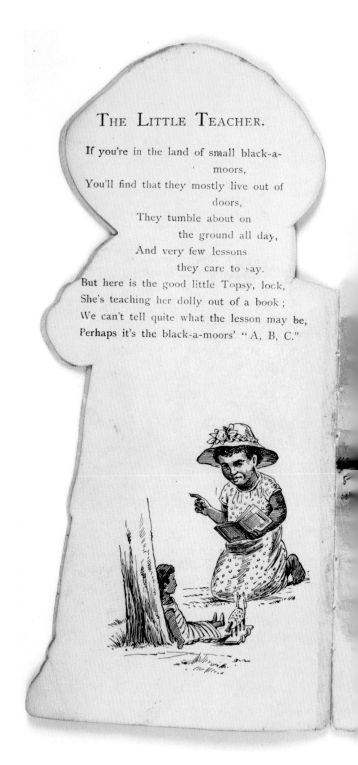

THE LITTLE TEACHER.

If you're in the land of small black-a-
moors,
You'll find that they mostly live out of
doors,
They tumble about on
the ground all day,
And very few lessons
they care to say.
But here is the good little Topsy, look,
She's teaching her dolly out of a book;
We can't tell quite what the lesson may be,
Perhaps it's the black-a-moors' " A, B, C."

"When I have got him out
I'll put him in de pail."

Cat. 97. *Topsy*, ca. 1894.

Seven Little Niggers chopping up sticks;
One chopped himself in halves, and then
there were Six.

**Cat. 98. *Ten Little
Niggers*, 1894.**

McLoughlin Brothers and Its Competitors

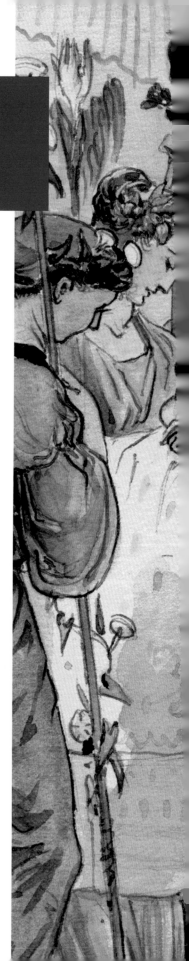

In nineteenth-century America, the publishing business was highly competitive as companies worked to capture the dollars being spent on books by the nation's swiftly growing middle class. Mcloughlin Brothers, with John McLoughlin Jr. at the helm, was always striving to put its juvenile books in the hands of more children than any other book producer. McLoughlin Brothers maintained a home office in New York City and built an enormous network of salesmen who distributed its books using wholesale resellers in cities from Boston to Chicago to San Francisco. The firm was very aware of demand, producing a large inventory of affordable and colorful picture books for children, and offered endless variations of designs and sizes in order to reach the highest number of consumers.

But McLoughlin Brothers wasn't the only publisher of picture books seeking market share. By 1893, its office in Manhattan was quite literally surrounded by more than forty other publishers, including large American firms like E. P. Dutton & Company and Hurd & Houghton, and transatlantic publishers such as the London-based Thomas Nelson & Sons. One reporter quipped, "Fifth Avenue below Twenty-third Street in New York is rapidly becoming the American Pasternoster Row," referring to the famous district in London that was the home of the printing district in that city.[13]

The McLoughlin brothers used a myriad of strategies to stay ahead of the competition, not all of them admirable. They blatantly copied foreign books, putting their own imprint on titles designed and written in England and then sold them for much less than the imported originals. They bought out rivals, or assumed their debts and negotiated advantageous settlement terms that often resulted in their competition getting out of juvenile publishing altogether. They pursued litigation if they felt one of their copyrights or patents had been infringed upon and were ruthless in their legal wrangling, taking one case all the way to the Supreme Court in 1903. In a note to customers in their trade catalog for that year, the brothers stated: "We must request all who use our goods to be on the lookout for counterfeits and to report them to us wherever found, so that we may take any needful steps to protect the interests of our customers and ourselves."[14] During the 1870 to 1880 period, McLoughlin Brothers became one of the most formidable publishers of the era, outpacing most of their competition in production, price, and distribution.

Cat. 119. "Fairies granting favors to Princess Desiree," ca. 1876.

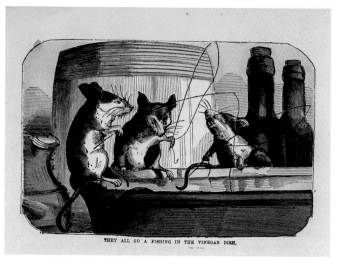

THEY ALL GO A FISHING IN THE VINEGAR DISH.

Cat. 100. *Eventful History of Three Little Mice,* 1858, left.
Cat. 102. *Three Blind Mice,* ca. 1863, above.

100. EVENTFUL HISTORY OF THREE LITTLE MICE AND HOW THEY BECAME BLIND. Good Child's Library Series. Illustrations by Winslow Homer. Stereotyped by J. E. Farwell & Co. Boston: E. O. Libby & Co., 1858.

101. EVENTFUL HISTORY OF THREE LITTLE MICE WHO RAN AFTER THE FARMER'S WIFE. Every Child's Own Book Series. London: Dean & Son, ca. 1859.

Loaned by Linda F. and Julian L. Lapides.

102. THE THREE BLIND MICE. Aunt Jenny's Series. New York: McLoughlin Brothers, 1863–1870.

Gift of Herbert H. Hosmer, 1978.

These three examples of books recounting the story behind the familiar nursery rhyme "Three Blind Mice" serve as an example of the fluidity with which images and texts moved back and forth across the Atlantic Ocean during the nineteenth century. The 1858 edition was published in Boston with illustrations designed by Winslow Homer (1836–1910). Homer, then in his twenties, created illustrations for over a dozen children's books as a young artist. He depicted the mice fishing in a basin of vinegar into which they would soon fall, resulting in their blindness. By October 1859, the book had been pirated by Dean & Son in London, who copied all the illustrations and sold the title for one shilling.[15] Three years later, McLoughlin Brothers put out its own version of the tale in the Aunt Jenny's Series, copying either the Libby or the Dean & Son version.

103. LITTLE RED RIDING HOOD. Our Favorite Fairy Tales Series. New York: Sheldon & Co., 1864.

Gift of Herbert H. Hosmer, 1978.

104. AUNT JENNY'S NURSERY RHYMES. New York: Hurd & Houghton, 1864–1865.

Gift of Herbert H. Hosmer, 1978.

105. SUNSHINE ABC BOOK. Cincinnati: Peter G. Thomson, between 1877 and 1884.

Gift of Herbert H. Hosmer, 1978.
Image, p. 21.

McLoughlin Brothers took its American competition seriously, especially when the quality was high and the pricing was affordable. These three books of traditional rhymes and stories were sold in bookshops around the country right alongside McLoughlin titles. All of these volumes were once part of the McLoughlin Brothers reference archive, showing that the firm kept a careful eye on its competitors' products. The Sheldon & Company *Little Red Riding Hood* was heavily marked up for copying by McLoughlin and is covered with inky fingerprints from pressmen working with the book on the press floor. Most of the images and the text were repurposed by McLoughlin for an 1875 edition of the fairytale published as part of its anthology *Old Stories for the Young*. The image of the Pied Piper from inside the Hurd & Houghton title appears in several nursery books published by McLoughlin Brothers starting in the 1860s, and the original watercolor (cat. 37) was part of the firm's art archive. Finally, Cincinnati-based publisher Peter G. Thomson (1851–1931) ran a very successful bookshop and lithographic printing office. Knowing that McLoughlin Brothers was aware of his growing standing in the market for children's books, the wily Thomson traveled to New York and agreed to get out of the business forever if McLoughlin bought him out, which the brothers did for $100,000 in 1884.

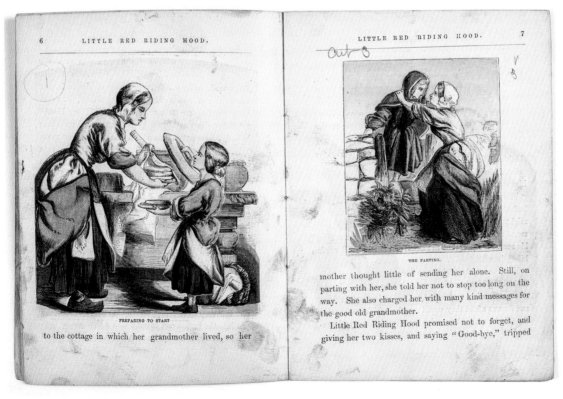

Cat. 103.
***Little Red Riding Hood,* 1864.**

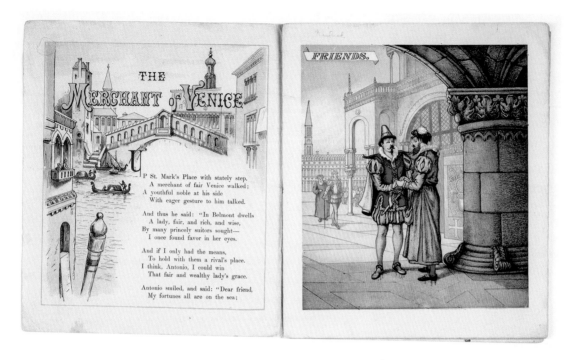

Cat. 110.
The Merchant of Venice, 1884.

106. **CENICENTILLA Ó EL ESCARPIN DE CRISTAL. Serie Nueva de Novelitas para Diversion é Instruccion de la Infancia. New York: D. Appleton & Co., publisher, printed by McLoughlin Brothers, ca. 1864.**

107. **LA CENICIENTA Ó EL ZAPITO DE VIDRIO. Serie Cuentos Pintados Para Niños. New York: D. Appleton & Co., publisher, printed by McLoughlin Brothers, 1867.**
Loaned by the George M. Fox Collection of Early Children's Books, Book Arts & Special Collections Center, San Francisco Public Library.
Image, p. 16.

108. **CINDERELLA OR THE GLASS SLIPPER. Cinderella Series. New York: McLoughlin Brothers, ca. 1863–1869.**
Gift of Herbert H. Hosmer, 1978.

McLoughlin Brothers could work collaboratively with a competitor when it suited the bottom line. In the 1860s, the firm quietly entered into a successful arrangement with D. Appleton & Company to manufacture picture books with Spanish text for sale in Latin America. Some of the earliest picture books manufactured by McLoughlin for Appleton told the tale of Cinderella. Although copyrighted in 1864, the wood blocks for the hand-colored illustrations were likely produced a decade or two before. An English-language version reusing some of the same wood engravings was also issued by McLoughlin Brothers.

109. **James C. Beard. LITTLE WORKERS: A HISTORY OF SOME OF GOD'S LITTLE CREATURES THAT LABOR WITHOUT HANDS. New York: R. Shugg & Co., 1871.**
Gift of Herbert H. Hosmer, 1978.

110. **Laura Valentine. THE MERCHANT OF VENICE. Little Folks Shakespeare Series. Cincinnati: Peter G. Thomson, 1884.**

After McLoughlin Brothers became a success, it quickly became a target. Two American competitors who went toe-to-toe with McLoughlin were Richard

Cat. 111.
Bow Wow! Or Dog Stories,
ca. 1888.

Shugg (1831–1904) in New York and Peter G. Thomson in Cincinnati, Ohio. Shugg moved into the old McLoughlin Brothers office at 30 Beekman Street, where he adopted the McLoughlin strategy of focusing solely on the juvenile market, publishing picture books, alphabet cards, games, and toy money. He eagerly embraced lithography, especially in big folio-size children's books, like this copy of the natural history book *Little Workers*.

Peter G. Thomson pirated his edition of the Shakespeare classic *Merchant of Venice* directly from an 1882 picture book published by McLoughlin Brothers. He also issued valentines, toy books, games, and paper dolls, and by 1880 was swiftly gaining market share in the Midwest. According to the Thomson family historian, McLoughlin Brothers was quick to view Thomson as a tangible threat and began "a campaign of price-cutting and coercion tactics among the retail dealers, in the hope of driving Peter out of business."[16]

111. Bow Wow! or Dog Stories. The Bow-Wow Series. London and Edinburgh: Thomas Nelson and Sons, 1888–1889.
Gift of Herbert H. Hosmer, 1978.

This picture book was once part of McLoughlin Brothers' reference archive and could have been purchased by the brothers at Thomas Nelson & Sons' New York shop, located just a block away from McLoughlin's downtown office. The pale shades of yellow, blue, and brown used in the images were typical of British book illustration in the late nineteenth century and are a far cry from the vivid reds and blues favored by McLoughlin Brothers. Thomas Nelson & Sons issued four pet-centric titles in the Bow-Wow Series, all offered on paper for six pennies or, like this one, on linen (deemed by the publisher "untearable" by small children) for one shilling. Juvenile publishing—what Nelson & Sons called "charming books for the little ones"—was just a small part of its book business, as they primarily sold editions of Shakespeare, gift books, novels, and longer titles for advanced readers.

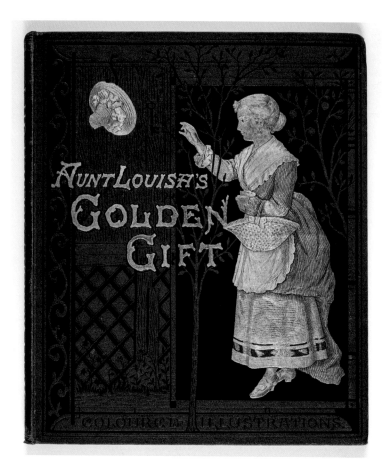

Cat. 114.
*Aunt Louisa's
Golden Gift,*
1875.

112. SING A SONG OF SIX PENCE. Aunt Friendly's Coloured Picture Books Series. London: F. Warne & Co., between 1865 and 1875.
Gift of Herbert H. Hosmer, 1978.

113. AUNT LOUISA'S HOME COMPANION. London: Frederick Warne & Co., and New York: Scribner, Welford, & Co., between 1868 and 1870.
Gift of Herbert H. Hosmer, 1978.

114. Laura Valentine, compiler. AUNT LOUISA'S GOLDEN GIFT. London: Frederick Warne & Co., 1875.
Gift of Herbert H. Hosmer, 1978.

These three volumes were all printed in London by Frederick Warne & Company and were preserved as part of the working archive of the McLoughlin Brothers firm, showing that the brothers were well aware of their competition in Europe. *Aunt Louisa's Golden Gift* was annotated by the company and includes a sheet layout diagram on one of the endpapers, evidence that McLoughlin staff attempted to reconstruct the sequence of printing from the book itself.

Beautiful British books like these were imported to the United States to satisfy the upper end of the children's market and were quickly pirated by McLoughlin Brothers (and others) and reissued to a wider public in cheaper formats. Although copyright laws existed in New York in this period, they were not extensively enforced and so pirated copies were common. The McLoughlin firm was blatant about its efforts, even boasting in its sales catalogs that its copies of British books were just as fine as the originals but could be bought at half the price.

Cat. 116.
Lazy Bones,
1860.

115. CINDERELLA. Aunt Louisa's Big Picture Series. New York: McLoughlin Brothers, ca. 1875.

This edition of *Cinderella* was part of the Aunt Louisa Big Picture Series issued by McLoughlin Brothers in an attempt to mimic the London publisher Frederick Warne's popular *Aunt Louisa London Toy Book*. At just twenty-five cents, this folio-sized series greatly underpriced the similarly-sized British imports offered by Warne, which retailed in England at five shillings, or about sixty cents.

116. Heinrich Hoffmann. LAZY BONES, OR FUNNY RHYMES WITH FUNNY PICTURES. London: Routledge, Warne & Routledge, 1860.
Gift of Herbert H. Hosmer, 1978.

117. Manuscript of LAZY BONES, OR FUNNY RHYMES WITH FUNNY PICTURES, n.d.
Gift of Herbert H. Hosmer, 1978.

The McLoughlin Brothers archive at the American Antiquarian Society includes many marked-up examples of its competitors' books, such as this one published in London. Printed before the Civil War, the story is a series of rhymes, each associated with a letter of the alphabet (the story spells out the name L-A-Z-Y B-O-N-E-S). The McLoughlin archive copy was annotated by McLoughlin staffers in preparation for creating a pirated edition: "Change to Negro with spear and shield" and "Make a good dandy out of this." These changes appear in stanzas fifty-eight and fifty-nine of the accompanying manuscript version, which would have been used by the editors and typesetters to lay out the text for the book. Marked-up copies and manuscript variations like these are evidence of the process behind the production of pirated editions of picture books issued by McLoughlin Brothers.

Cats. 118 & 120. *Hind in the Wood*, 1875, and "The Prince hunts the white hind," ca. 1876.

118. Marie-Catherine Aulnoy. THE HIND IN THE WOOD. Schilling Series. London & New York: George Routledge & Sons, 1875.
Gift of Herbert H. Hosmer, 1978.

119. After Walter Crane. "Fairies granting favors to Princess Desiree while the Fairy of the Fountain looks on." From HIND IN THE WOOD. Watercolor, pen and ink, ca. 1876.
Gift of Herbert H. Hosmer, 1978.
Image, pp. 98-99.

120. After Walter Crane. "The Prince hunts the white hind." From HIND IN THE WOOD. Watercolor, pen and ink, ca. 1876.
Gift of Herbert H. Hosmer, 1978.

121. Marie-Catherine Aulnoy. FAWN IN THE WOOD. Yellow Dwarf Series. New York: McLoughlin Brothers, 1882.

A set of finely executed watercolors are preserved as part of the art archives of the McLoughlin Brothers firm at the American Antiquarian Society. They were copied by an unidentified illustrator from images originally created by British artist Walter Crane (1845–1915) for an edition of the classic fairy tale *Hind in the Wood* published in London in 1875. Around 1882, McLoughlin Brothers produced *Fawn in the Wood*, a competitive and completely pirated edition of this tale (abbreviated significantly) for the American market. McLoughlin's book sold for a fraction of the price of the original *Hind in the Wood*. Walter Crane famously complained about unauthorized McLoughlin reproductions of another book, *The Baby's Opera*, in an 1877 letter to the editor of *Scribner's Monthly*. He wrote, "The pirated edition, a copy of which I have seen, grossly misrepresents my drawings both in style and coloring . . . the full page colored plates are complete travesties." It was not until the American Copyright Law of 1891 that the rights of foreign copyright holders were respected in the U.S.

122. William Cowper. THE DIVERTING HISTORY OF JOHN GILPIN. R. Caldecott's Picture Books Series. London: George Routledge & Sons, 1881.
Gift of Herbert H. Hosmer, 1978.

123. William Cowper. THE DIVERTING HISTORY OF JOHN GILPIN. Caldecott Award Series. New York: McLoughlin Brothers, ca. 1881.
Gift of Herbert H. Hosmer, 1978.

The story of John Gilpin and his runaway horse was a perennial favorite with children in England and America (cat. 5). Rather than create original art for this circa 1881 printing of the tale, McLoughlin Brothers copied exactly the illustrations made in England by famed artist Randolph Caldecott (1846–1886), brightening up the colors and then lowering the price of the book in order to undercut the British title being imported into the United States. Caldecott's work was well known in America and was in heavy demand during the 1881 holiday season. One reviewer noted "the evident leaning of public fancy toward the Greenaway-Caldecott style of illustrated juveniles, the majority of publishers showing on their lists one or more of this attractive class of picture books."[17] McLoughlin even created a new series, The Caldecott Award, to capitalize on the notoriety of Randolph Caldecott.

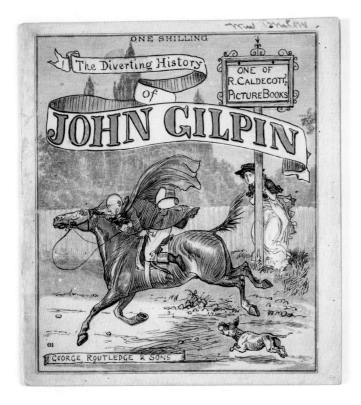
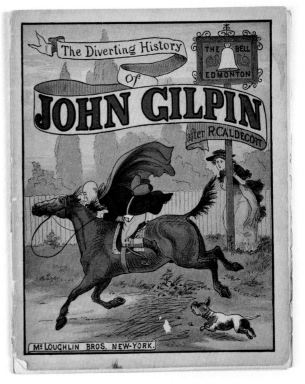

Cats. 122 & 123. *The Diverting History of John Gilpin, ca. 1881.*

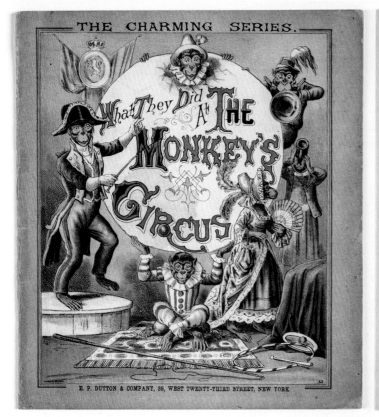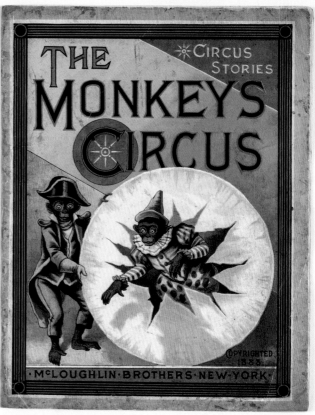

Cats. 124 & 125. *What They Did at the Monkey's Circus* and *The Monkeys Circus*, 1883.

124. WHAT THEY DID AT THE MONKEY'S CIRCUS. Charming Series. New York: E. P. Dutton & Co., 1883.

Gift of Herbert H. Hosmer, 1978.

125. THE MONKEYS CIRCUS. Circus Stories Series. New York: McLoughlin Brothers, 1883.

Gift of Ruth Adomeit.

American publishers not only purloined content and design of books from their transatlantic competitors, but also from each other. Founded in Boston, publisher E. P. Dutton moved to New York in 1868 where it published, among other things, lengthy juvenile novels and religious literature. This pair of titles illustrates that Dutton also competed directly against McLoughlin Brothers in the picture book market. These two versions of the same tale were published in the same year. On the back cover of its book, Dutton emphasized its cultured approach to literature for children, saying, "These have been especially designed and printed in the best and most artistic manner. . . . No book in any of our different series contains anything approaching vulgarity—The Publisher's aim being to furnish amusement, coupled with refinement, for our dear little ones." McLoughlin copyrighted its version of the book and described it as "very showy" while also stating, "These books will surprise and delight the little ones." Dutton charged twenty-five cents retail for its copy. McLoughlin charged fifteen cents. It is unknown which version hit the market first.

126. Lydia L. A. Very. Goody Two Shoes. Boston: Louis Prang & Co., ca. 1863–1865.

There are many ways to beat the competition in business and not all have to do with products and design. Disrupting distribution channels such as sales teams and networks is also an effective strategy, and was one practiced by McLoughlin Brothers. Although Louis Prang & Company's Boston printing business mainly focused on prints, greeting cards, and chromolithographed ephemera, it also made picture books like this small shaped book, which would have sold alongside McLoughlin Brothers toy books. Prang issued more than thirty books for young readers between 1861 and 1890, including four shaped books written by Massachusetts poet Lydia L. A. Very (1823–1901). The books were distributed by Prang's growing network of traveling salesmen, who carried large sample books full of Prang products on visits to stationers, booksellers, and merchants across the country, building important relationships that translated into profits. In 1881, McLoughlin Brothers hired away one of Prang's most experienced salesmen, John H. Black (d. 1908), employing him to build up its own national distribution network.

127. The Three Kittens. Printed in Bavaria. New York: E. P. Dutton & Co., and London: Ernest Nister, 1895.
Gift of Herbert H. Hosmer, 1978.

McLoughlin Brothers frequently took its American and European competitors to court, vigorously defending its own patents and copyright filings. In 1890, E. P. Dutton & Company became the American representative for English and Bavarian picture book publisher Ernest Nister (1841–1906), a fruitful partnership that would last until 1914. In an effort to confine this competition, which it perceived as a threat to its own expansion, in 1896 McLoughlin Brothers sued E. P. Dutton & Company for "importing books in violation of section 3 of the International Copyright Law." The details of the case, which was won by McLoughlin Brothers, stated that although Nister's books were marked "copyrighted" on the covers, no payments to the United States government had been made to register the foreign titles.[18]

McLoughlin Brothers' Steady Sellers

A t the Centennial Exhibition in Philadelphia in 1876, McLoughlin Brothers displayed a large glass-front case of its goods which was described by one reporter as full of "their popular toy-books, in brilliant color plates and with chromo bindings, card games and blocks and games."[19] Ten million visitors streamed through the exhibition that year, and those that took a moment to peer into the case would have seen some of the firm's steady sellers—books like *Robinson Crusoe* and *Cinderella* that the brothers sold consistently over decades, as well as nursery rhymes and religious stories that were always in demand. These books formed the backbone of the inventory of McLoughlin Brothers and, while constantly updated and refreshed, came to be expected by the firm's customer base.

McLoughlin Brothers published an enormous quantity of books for children—scholars estimate about 1,000 titles appeared in over 150 different series—using its experience and talents to feed the demand for affordable books for children while also anticipating market trends. Once a book was established as a steady seller, the company continued to reissue it, reformat it, dress it up or down, and promote it across formats from penny books to deluxe editions, on card games and board games, or as paper dolls. They also kept up with fads and trends, featuring prominent illustrators such as Thomas Nast and introducing up-to-date novelty games and popular amusements.

The bookselling business became more competitive as the end of the nineteenth century approached. Hundreds of independent bookshops opened across the country to serve the demands of a growing population. Thirty-eight million people lived in the United States in 1870. By 1900 that number had nearly doubled to 76.2 million, and most of these were readers. In 1870, 20 percent of Americans over the age of 14 could not read. By 1900, that figure had dropped to 10 percent. McLoughlin Brothers consistently offered a steady supply of fairytales, easy readers, and holiday books to help meet the demand of a more literate and growing populace.

Cat. 140. *Mother Goose's Magic Transformations*, ca. 1882.

128. Thomas Nast. Mock up for Robinson Crusoe with printed insertions from Nast's Illustrated Almanac for 1871, 1870.

129. Robinson Crusoe. New York: McLoughlin Brothers, 1895.
Gift of Herbert H. Hosmer, 1978.

Retellings of Daniel Defoe's *Robinson Crusoe* were commonplace in the United States throughout the nineteenth century. By 1860, McLoughlin Brothers was offering versions of the story in multiple formats. For picture books, the firm pared the narrative down substantially and focused on Crusoe's interactions with animals on the island or his friendship with Friday. Told with silhouette-style illustration and rhyming verse, this mock up for a picture book co-opted whole sections from Thomas Nast's first comic almanac, published by McLoughlin Brothers in 1870. The almanac was a sensation, selling 36,000 copies in two weeks.[20] The popularity of the almanac inspired McLoughlin to reuse the silhouette illustrations augmented with full-page additions (also by Nast) to create a *Robinson Crusoe* picture book. The mock up, part of the business library of the firm, illustrates the often imprecise compilation and design process behind the making of books in the nineteenth century.

Over twenty years later, in 1895, *Crusoe* was still a top seller and McLoughlin used the story to show off its latest style of picture book printing. *Robinson Crusoe* got a new cast as a proto-action figure in a shaped book edition of the classic tale from 1895, which the firm also took care to copyright. This edition was highly abbreviated for younger children and sold for fifteen cents. It was produced on modern chromolithographic presses newly installed in the firm's Brooklyn factory. McLoughlin Brothers continued to produce editions of Defoe's classic well into the twentieth century.

Cat. 132. *The Prodigal Son,* **1882.**

130. Artist unknown. "Madonna and Child." Watercolor, pen and ink, ca. 1900.

131. Isaac Watts. Early Religion. Watts' Songs Series. New York: McLoughlin Brothers, 1870.
Gift of Herbert H. Hosmer, 1978.

132. Henry William Dulyken. The Prodigal Son. Golden Light Series. New York: McLoughlin Brothers, 1882.
Gift of Herbert H. Hosmer, 1978.

133. Mrs. Grive. Moses and the Wanderings of the Children of Israel. Half Hours with the Bible, Second Series. New York: McLoughlin Brothers, 1886.
Gift of Herbert H. Hosmer, 1978.

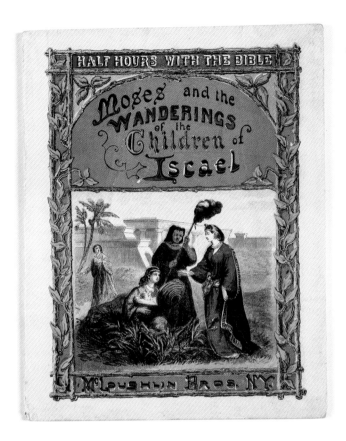

Cat. 133.
***Moses and the Wanderings of the Children of Israel,* 1886.**

Religious publications were a bread-and-butter part of the book business for McLoughlin Brothers, as they were for other publishers of the era. Sunday Schools, religious organizations, and parents all purchased illustrated Christian story books to help educate and inculcate children. Hundreds of original illustrations, such as the Madonna and child watercolor, were made for religious picture books and now reside in the American Antiquarian Society's McLoughlin Brothers art archive. These were used and reused in stories and parables from both the Old and the New Testaments, including those of the prodigal son, Noah and the ark, the good Samaritan, and Moses.

The firm's 1870 sales catalog included early printings of all three of the titles gathered here. McLoughlin offered a series of six picture book versions of Isaac Watts's *Divine Songs for Children*, bringing Watts's eighteenth-century religious poetry into the visually oriented children's book market of the late nineteenth century. These inexpensive titles sold for five cents each. The Golden Light Series, including *The Prodigal Son*, which was pirated from a British book written by famed author and translator H. W. Dulyken, sold for twenty cents in the same catalog. The identity of "Mrs. Grive," who is credited as author on many of McLoughlin's religious titles, has not been determined and is likely a pseudonym. A dozen titles in the series Half Hours with the Bible bear this name on the cover or title page. The books tackle everything from biblical history and parables to more difficult subjects, including the resurrection and the role of Jesus in Christian life. Watts's series, the Golden Light books, and Grive's titles all appear in McLoughlin catalogs as steady sellers—reissued, repackaged, and updated until 1900.

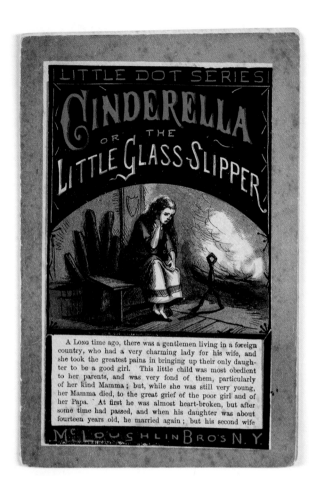

Cat. 135.
Cinderella or the
Little Glass Slipper,
1875.

134. HOP O' MY THUMB. CINDERELLA. Aunt
Lulu's Series. New York: McLoughlin
Brothers, 1867.

Gift of Herbert H. Hosmer, 1978.

135. CINDERELLA OR THE LITTLE GLASS
SLIPPER. Little Dot Series. New York:
McLoughlin Brothers, 1875.

Gift of Herbert H. Hosmer, 1978.

136. CINDERELLA OR THE LITTLE GLASS
SLIPPER. Red Riding Hood Series. Plate
house copy. New York: McLoughlin
Brothers, 1896.

These three editions of *Cinderella* show how
McLoughlin tinkered with, marketed, and
remarketed a popular fairy tale for decades. In the case
of the 1867 Aunt Lulu's Series, a version of *Cinderella*
originally published separately was reissued in a folio-
format anthology with *Hop O' My Thumb*, *Aladdin*, and
Sleeping Beauty, with each tale taking up two pages.
The illustrations were sloppily hand-colored. The very
same illustrations were reused eight years later in the
Little Dot Series. Retailing at just one cent, this book
was at the very lowest price point in the McLoughlin
Brothers output, so it is no surprise that beyond the color
printed title page, the illustrations are not colored at
all. The linen-backed, "indestructible" 1896 edition is a
McLoughlin Brothers press room plate house copy with
editorial annotations. It was housed in the firm's library
so that it could be consulted during re-publication or if
the title was slated to be updated.

137. JUANILLO BOCADO. **Mi Abuela Fácil Series. New York: D. Appleton, publisher, printed by McLoughlin Brothers, ca. 1870.**

138. ALÍ BABÁ Ó LOS CUARENTA LADRONES. **Novelitas de las Maravillas Series. Plate house copy. New York: D. Appleton, publisher, printed by McLoughlin Brothers, ca. 1891.**

139. Manuscript draft of ALÍ BABÁ Ó LOS CUARENTA LADRONES.

Around 1865, McLoughlin Brothers entered into a long-term business arrangement with its competitors D. Appleton & Company, also in New York, to publish Spanish-language books for children. McLoughlin did the printing and Appleton distributed the titles to customers in Mexico, South America, and Cuba. Other titles in the series included *Robinson Crusoe*, *The White Cat*, and *Cinderella* (cats. 106, 107). This relationship lasted into the twentieth century, indicating that the Spanish-language picture books were steady sellers. Spanish-language printings of classic tales like

Ali Baba and Mother Goose were constantly updated by both firms. The manuscript draft from the McLoughlin Brothers archives was housed with the plate house copy.

140. "Jack and Jill." From MOTHER GOOSE'S MAGIC TRANSFORMATIONS. **Transformation Toy Books Series. Illustrations by Justin Howard. New York: McLoughlin Brothers, ca. 1882.**
Image, pp. 110-111.

In the 1880s, McLoughlin Brothers offered multiple types of mechanical books, which quickly became steady sellers. Some popped up, others had pull tabs. This Mother Goose volume was made up of illustrations with flaps. Each flap could be folded back to show progressive stages of the narrative. This volume sold for twenty-five cents in 1882 and was promoted as a "transformation toy book." Many of these mechanical books were patented by the firm in an attempt to protect the construction design and safeguard McLoughlin Brothers' market position as a leader in the field of innovative toy books and games.

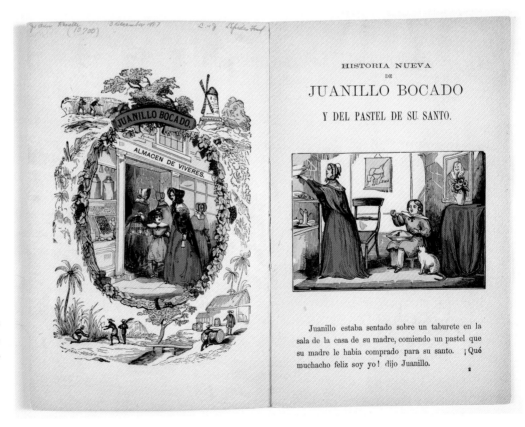

Cat. 137.
Juanillo Bocado,
ca. 1870.

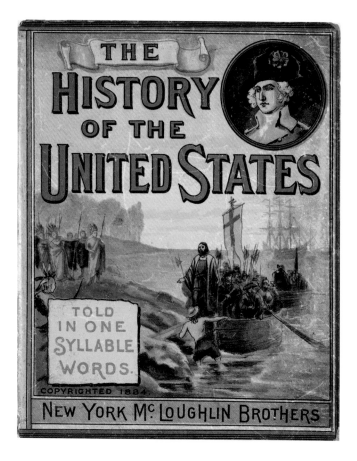

Cat. 142.
The History of the
United States Told In
One Syllable Words, ca. 1884.

141. Josephine Pollard. Our Hero General U.S. Grant. New York: McLoughlin Brothers, ca. 1885.

Gift of Herbert H. Hosmer, 1978.

142. Josephine Pollard. The History of the United States Told in One Syllable Words. New York: McLoughlin Brothers, ca. 1884.

Gift of Herbert H. Hosmer, 1978.

McLoughlin Brothers published many steady sellers with purely American content. In the early 1880s, the firm hired New York author Josephine Pollard (1834–1892) to produce a series of easy readers for beginners focused on American subjects. A famed poet and author, Pollard also wrote hymns and articles for the religious periodical press. She perfected the process of distilling biographies and histories down to simple language for beginners. As early as 1867, McLoughlin Brothers included easy readers in its book line, but the firm really expanded into this market in the late 1880s with Pollard's efforts.

The biography of Ulysses S. Grant (1822–1885), issued the year of his death, sold for one dollar. It was highlighted in several advertisements taken out by McLoughlin Brothers in the fall of 1885, as the firm rushed to get the book ready for the holiday market. The company's competitor, George Routledge & Son, issued a "words of one syllable" compilation of the *Lives of the Presidents* that same season.[21] Pollard's titles remained steady sellers for more than a decade and included a one-syllable *Life of Washington*, books about different sports, and natural history texts (cat. 146).

143. WONDERLAND STORIES. New York: McLoughlin Brothers, 1897.

Gift of Herbert H. Hosmer, 1978.

Although Washington Irving's *Rip Van Winkle* was originally published in 1819, the time-traveling Dutch New Yorker became a staple of McLoughlin picture books starting in the 1860s. The story was updated and reprinted repeatedly (cats. 164, 165), indicating that it likely sold well to American customers. Many parts of Irving's story lend themselves to the picture book format, including the nine-pins scene, where Rip bowls with mysterious elf-like creatures. The color illustrations in this edition were created on large steam-powered lithographic presses in the firm's Brooklyn factory, not far from where Irving originally wrote his *Knickerbocker* stories.

144. Attributed to Charles Kendrick. "Moll Pitcher at the Battle of Monmouth." Watercolor, ca. 1900.

145. Attributed to Charles Kendrick. "Gen. Putnam's Escape from the British." Watercolor, ca. 1900.

American history provided subject matter for any number of steady-selling picture books for McLoughlin Brothers. This pair of action-packed watercolors propagated the stories on which the nation's history would be based. Molly Pitcher loads her husband's cannon during a battle in New Jersey, representing all of the valiant women who helped fight the British during the American Revolution. The story of General Israel Putnam's 1779 escape from British forces in Greenwich, Connecticut, was frequently retold in McLoughlin Brothers picture books (cat. 66) and

Cats. 144 & 145.
***Moll Pitcher at the Battle of Monmouth* and *Gen. Putnam's Escape from the British,* ca. 1900.**

usually featured Putnam's daring ride down a steep path or stairs. It is unknown whether these watercolors from the McLoughlin Brothers archives, which are attributed to Charles Kendrick (d. 1914), were made on speculation or were produced for a specific publication. Kendrick worked as a periodical illustrator and also made illustrations for McLoughlin's competitor R. Worthington & Company.

146. Josephine Pollard. Small Birds. Bird and Animal Series. New York: McLoughlin Brothers, 1886.
Gift of Herbert H. Hosmer, 1978.

147. Artist unknown. Cover design for Small Birds. Watercolor and graphite, ca. 1886.

Natural history books were popular with children and their parents after the Civil War as discoveries in biology and evolution became more accepted around the world during the latter portion of the century. This title is one of a series of six natural history picture books for young children focused on animal life, including *Small Animals*, *Game Animals*, and *Wild Animals*. McLoughlin Brothers copyrighted each book in an effort to control pirated copies. *Small Birds*, along with the entire Bird and Animal Series, was still being offered by the company in 1903. The original watercolor design for the cover is preserved in the business archives and includes color notations on the front and an inscription on the back: "For Spanish covers / Yellow, Red & black of top piece. Black letters only to set into the ribbon. Change firm's name to red letters." No copies of a Spanish-language version have been located to date.

148. The Babes in the Wood. Young Folks Series. Illustrations by Richard André. New York: McLoughlin Brothers, 1888.
Gift of Herbert H. Hosmer, 1978.

149. Little Folks Cubes: The Babes in the Wood. Illustrations by Richard André. New York: McLoughlin Brothers, 1888.

McLoughlin Brothers frequently cross-promoted its best-selling children's books with its line of games. These cube blocks depicting scenes from the well-known tale *The Babes in the Wood* are covered with the exact chromolithographs that acted as plates in the book version of the story, available for purchase at the same time. Many McLoughlin paper dolls, board games, toy panoramas (cat. 165), and card games were related to the firm's popular stories and books, a strategy that allowed the firm to reuse expensive artwork and illustrations and to promote products across formats.

150. William Bruton. Young Artist Painting Book. New York: McLoughlin Brothers, after 1882.
Gift of Herbert H. Hosmer, 1978.
Image, frontispiece.

151. Chiromagica. New York: McLoughlin Brothers, ca. 1872.
Image, cover.

Many of McLoughlin Brothers' non-picture book products were also steady sellers. Even though competitors in Philadelphia and Europe had been selling them for over a decade, painting and coloring books were not introduced by McLoughlin until 1882. These volumes sold for just ten cents each and were touted by the firm in its 1882 catalog as "an unfailing source of amusement for children. They instruct and refine, while giving pleasure, and aid in developing any talent they may have." With illustrations by staff artist William Bruton, this example contains scenes of American children at play and includes a series of advertisements on the back cover for games sold by McLoughlin Brothers.

The company's *Chiromagica* toy was offered by the company for more than a decade, starting around 1872, and was heavily promoted in its trade catalogs and advertisements during that time. Controlled by carefully placed magnets, players asked this fortune-

Cats. 148 & 149. *The Babes in the Wood* **book and puzzle, 1888.**

telling game questions and then placed discs on the glass-topped board—the pointer would magically spin to reveal the correct answer. The game was not inexpensive, selling for two dollars in 1879. In 1894, one copy was owned by a boys' club in New Haven, Connecticut, run by a minister who wrote about the homeless street boys that he served, "They are reading good books, and the games are in all cases innocent and in some cases helpful, such as the dissected maps and Chiromagica, which is a wheel answering questions in geography, history, etc."[22]

152. Clement Clarke Moore. A Visit from St. Nicholas. Illustrations by Thomas Nast. New York: McLoughlin Brothers, 1869.

153. Clement Clarke Moore. The Night Before Christmas or A Visit of St. Nicholas. Plate house copy. New York: McLoughlin Brothers, 1888.
Gift of Herbert H. Hosmer, 1978.
Image, p. 37.

154. Artist unknown. Cover design for The Night Before Christmas. Watercolor, pen and ink, gouache, ca. 1888.
Gift of Herbert H. Hosmer, 1978.

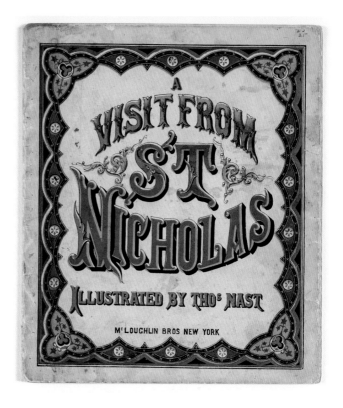

Cat. 152. *A Visit from St. Nicholas, 1869.*

McLoughlin Brothers is well known for creating picture books associated with Christmas, and its branding of products for the holiday season was ambitious, starting with one of their first holiday books in 1869. In that year the firm hired cartoonist Thomas Nast to create a picture book version of the poem *The Night Before Christmas*. Nast's illustrations, which combined the whimsical quality of the poem with humorous caricature, forever shaped America's cultural image of Santa Claus. In earlier children's books, Santa was represented by a range of types, including a thin, somber Saint Nicholas and a slightly ominous bearded peddler with a pack. In Nast's hands, Santa Claus became an elfin man in a fur suit whose cheery face and smoking pipe reflected a character who enjoyed both supernatural power and earthly pleasures.

The 1869 printing of McLoughlin Brothers' *A Visit from St. Nicholas* was a triumph and was in near-constant demand for over a decade. A pristine copy of this edition is very rare, as most copies were worn to pieces by eager young hands. Recognizing the poem's potential, the firm periodically issued updated versions featuring modern toys and style of dress. The plate house copy of an 1888 edition of *The Night Before Christmas*, along with the original watercolors used for its illustrations, was retained by the firm and was part of the art archive used for consultation during the design and republishing process.

Cat. 157.
Three Christmas Boxes, **1882.**

155. George P. Webster. Santa Claus & His Works. Cover illustration by Justin Howard, interior illustrations by Thomas Nast. New York: McLoughlin Brothers, ca. 1882.
Gift of Herbert H. Hosmer, 1978.

156. Christmas Boxes. New York: McLoughlin Brothers, 1881.

157. Three Christmas Boxes. Illustrations by William Bruton. New York: McLoughlin Brothers, 1882.
Gift of Herbert H. Hosmer, 1978.

McLoughlin Brothers was quick to capitalize on the potential of Santa-related books as

holiday commodities, contracting again with Nast for illustrations to accompany what was essentially a Santa sequel to *A Visit from St. Nicholas.* Nast created images for George Webster's poem *Santa Claus and His Works,* a story that reveals what Santa does in the off season. Reprinted annually for over a dozen years, Webster's poem describes "Santa Clausville" at the North Pole where the fur-clad elf makes toys and keeps track of good and bad children with a telescope.

Gradually McLoughlin built a mini-empire of steady-selling Santa products on the backs of the Nast books. They employed many illustrators to create a host of holiday-themed books like *The Christmas Boxes* (later retitled *Three Christmas Boxes*), a story set at Christmastime in which Santa plays a supporting role.

158. St. Nicholas. New York: McLoughlin Brothers, 1895.

Gift of Herbert H. Hosmer, 1978.

159. Illustration for St. Nicholas. Watercolor, pen and ink, ca. 1895.

Gift of Herbert H. Hosmer, 1978.

From the early nineteenth century, American publishers knew that children's books made excellent holiday gifts and almost every publisher in the country released a list of new titles in November especially designed for the holiday market. With its numerous Santa-centered books and toys, McLoughlin was instrumental in shifting the holiday market focus away from New Year's Day, which had been the dominant day of winter celebrations in the Early Republic, to Christmas.

One newspaper editor exclaimed in 1891, "Deluge the nurseries of this our happy land with toys and games, toy-books, such as those that McLoughlin Bros. provide every Christmas, in sheer excess of seasonable goodwill to mankind. Who ever dreamt of making a profit out of toys?"[23] McLoughlin Brothers clearly dreamed of profits, and found them abundantly in Christmas publishing. The ten-cent die-cut shaped book *St. Nicholas* is an anthology of poems, most having a Christmas theme. Published in 1895 as the company was switching over to lithographic presses for the majority of its production, the book is full of seasonal illustrations. The original watercolor drawings for the page layouts show the scenes connected by a loose border of toys, an abstract approach to illustration favored by McLoughlin in the 1890s.

160. Game of the Visit of Santa Claus. New York: McLoughlin Brothers, 1897.

Gift of Herbert H. Hosmer in memory of John Greene Chandler, 1985.

McLoughlin continued to capitalize on the Christmas market in 1898 by issuing *Game of the Visit of Santa Claus*. The game is designed so that players receive gifts from Santa as he flies in his sleigh around the board. The winner is the player who amasses the most gifts while having Santa skip over their opponents. This game celebrates the growing consumerism of the holiday and also surreptitiously conveys Santa's seal of approval for McLoughlin Brothers products, many of which are, not surprisingly, featured as the gifts delivered by St. Nick during the game.

161. Christmas Joys. New York: McLoughlin Brothers, 1899.

At the very end of the nineteenth century, McLoughlin Brothers published a grand gift book containing stories, poems, and a picture on nearly every page. Despite the cover design featuring a chromolithographed decal of Santa over a fireplace, the contents inside have nothing whatsoever to do with Christmas; the image of St. Nick was used solely to brand the book for the Christmas gift market. This strategy was used repeatedly by the firm on toys as well, with numerous sets of "Christmas blocks" and "Christmas puzzles," the contents of which were completely unconnected to the winter holiday, being offered for sale in October and November.

Cat. 160.
Game of the Visit of Santa Claus, 1897.

THE GOLDEN AGE OF McLOUGHLIN BROTHERS

Starting around 1880, McLoughlin Brothers entered an era of production and expansion that made it the largest and arguably the most significant distributor of children's literature in the nation. Its extensive factory in Brooklyn, which opened around 1870, reached capacity during this time, employing over 850 people and shipping books and games all over the world. The elaborate, colorful picture books and toys from this period are highly sought by collectors today and reflect a fin-de-siècle and early twentieth-century blossoming of design and innovation. The material produced during the golden age of the firm surpassed in every way the modest paper-bound editions from the first decade of McLoughlin Brothers. It was showier, more complex, contained more color, and used a wider variety of illustration styles.

The firm's product line expanded dramatically in this era. Steady sellers like Mother Goose and Struwwelpeter stories remained on the list of titles, but they were joined by many new offerings of innovative picture books, including flap books and pop-up books, as well as dozens of new toys and games for children. In 1908, McLoughlin Brothers crowed about its success in an advertisement designed to attract more wholesalers to carry and distribute its products: "One jealous thought we hold, and that is that our stock on every count, be it *price*, *quality* or *attractiveness*, shall always remain, what it always has been, second to none. The imprint of McLoughlin Brothers must continue on the best juvenile literature. The best artists, the best taste, the best material, the best processes, the best workmanship—all these factors conspire to impart strength of character to the line and endow it with a personal magnetism."[24]

McLoughlin Brothers products were everywhere in this period. They turned up in school curriculums, in homes for underprivileged youth, in middle-class parlors, and among elites. Market saturation and domination, a long-term goal of John McLoughlin Jr., was very nearly reached when McLoughlin Brothers' publishing empire was at its peak. As a result, because it became the most successful firm in the juvenile trade, the tables turned and McLoughlin Brothers products and technology started to be pirated by other publishers in America and Europe. A flurry of litigation ensued as McLoughlin executives sought to defend their long list of patents and copyright filings. Bookseller and stationer trade periodicals of this era are filled with news of court cases, settlements, and the legal wrangling of McLoughlin Brothers.

Even though the McLoughlin brothers were ahead of the curve when they decided in the 1850s to focus exclusively on publications for children, by the 1880s they were certainly not alone in doing so. Many distinguished publishers in this era expanded and improved their offerings for young readers. It made good business sense because that segment of the market was growing quickly. Writing in 1886, publisher Charles B. Shepard summed it up, "In the literature of this last quarter of the nineteenth century the rising generation is certainly not forgotten, and it seems to me to be one of the best signs of social progress that the making of books for our boys and girls has come to be so important a branch of the publishers' business, and to absorb so large a part of the best literary and artistic labor of the country."[25]

Cat. 166.
Winter, 1884.

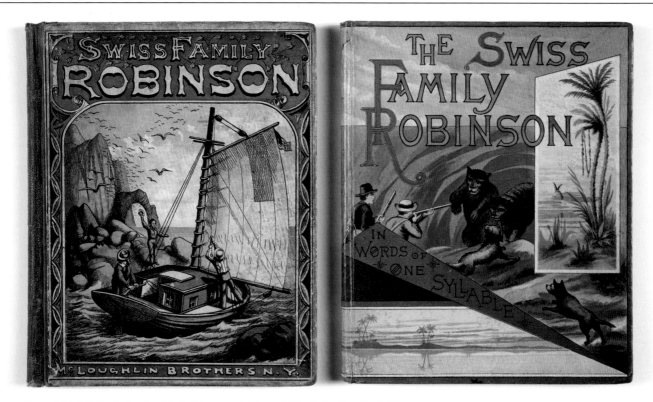

Cats. 162 & 163. *Swiss Family Robinson*, **1880, and** *The Swiss Family Robinson*, **1883.**

162. **Abridged by Isabella F. Mayo. THE SWISS FAMILY ROBINSON, IN WORDS OF ONE SYLLABLE. New York: McLoughlin Brothers, 1880.**

Gift of Herbert H. Hosmer, 1978.

163. **Abridged by Isabella F. Mayo. THE SWISS FAMILY ROBINSON, IN WORDS OF ONE SYLLABLE. New York: McLoughlin Brothers, 1883.**

Gift of Herbert H. Hosmer, 1978.

These abridged editions of *Swiss Family Robinson* were written in words of one syllable and were intended for beginning readers. Originally published in Switzerland in 1812, the first American edition of the tale of a castaway family was published in New York in 1832. McLoughlin Brothers steadily republished variant editions of the story for children between 1880 and 1910, including picture books, juvenile readers, and condensed versions. Considered side by side, this pair

of books illustrates how frequently the firm redesigned and repackaged its titles during the golden age. The 1880 cover harkens back to the 1870s in style, while the 1883 design updates the lettering and layout to reflect the art nouveau style then coming into vogue.

164. **"Hudson's Men and the Nine Pin Game." In AUNT LOUISA'S CHILD'S DELIGHT. Illustrated by Thomas Nast. New York: McLoughlin Brothers, ca. 1882.**

Gift of Herbert H. Hosmer, 1978.

165. **UNCLE SAM'S PANORAMA OF RIP VAN WINKLE AND YANKEE DOODLE. Illustrated by Thomas Nast. New York: McLoughlin Brothers, ca. 1875.**

The story "Rip Van Winkle" was first published in 1819 by American author Washington Irving. During its golden age, McLoughlin Brothers issued several deluxe editions of the popular American story for children, the earliest dating to 1869. Thomas Nast, the illustrator, based the likeness of Rip on the popular American stage actor Joseph Jefferson (1829–1905). Jefferson first played Rip in 1859 and continued to act the part for forty years, becoming completely associated with the role. McLoughlin Brothers capitalized on Jefferson's fame by using the actor's likeness (without credit) to also tell the story for children. The original picture book images were repurposed on a scroll toy theater issued by McLoughlin Brothers in 1875 and were repeatedly reused in books and toys into the 1880s.

166. WINTER. Little Showman's Series. New York: McLoughlin Brothers, 1884.
Gift of Herbert H. Hosmer, 1978.
Image, pp. 124-125.

167. JUMBO AND THE COUNTRYMAN. Little Showman's Series. New York: McLoughlin Brothers, 1886.

These elaborate pop-up books were each issued as part of a series and were offered in two sizes during the firm's golden age. *Winter* was one of four books that depicted the seasons of the year (sold for fifty cents each), and *Jumbo* was one of six books that featured animals in a zoo (twenty-five cents each). The books open along one bound edge and have a poem printed below a three-dimensional scene that functions as a sort of peep show to illustrate the verse. The ten titles hit the market at the same time in late 1883 and were touted by McLoughlin as "the novelty of the season." The firm described the products in an advertisement: "If you visit a store where these books are spread out on the counters, and raise their covers, the likeness to a book will end with a charming surprise. Beautiful Tableaux will magically appear, Cages of Wild Animals will spring into being, and while you are gratifying your own curiosity, you will find yourself acting the part of the showman, and all the customers, particularly the little ones, will be flocking around to see the Show."[26]

Cat. 165. *Uncle Sam's Panorama of Rip Van Winkle and Yankee Doodle,* **ca. 1875.**

Cat. 169. *Robinson Crusoe,* **1893.**

168. Aladdin or the Wonderful Lamp. Pantomime Toy Books. New York: McLoughlin Brothers, 1882.

169. Robinson Crusoe. New York: McLoughlin Brothers, 1893.
Gift of Herbert H. Hosmer, 1978.

This pair of books illustrates one of the innovations employed by McLoughlin Brothers in the 1880s and 1890s—creating books that looked like small theaters. In the 1880s, the books were a standard square or rectangular format on the outside, and by 1891 the firm had introduced a shaped version. Inside, the stories were told with minimal text and pictorial flaps. Audience members in theater boxes printed on the inner boards watch the story unfold as the reader lifts left and right flaps in different combinations, as they wish. The books,

which cost between thirty-five and fifty cents, apparently sold very well. In November 1891, a trade journal noted, "McLoughlin Brothers have placed on the market a line of shaped pantomime books which are very interesting and which will be rapid sellers as Christmas souvenirs. These books are miniature stages, on which are played 'Cinderella,' 'Little Red Riding Hood,' and other children's favorites."[27]

170. "The Parrot Girl." In Naughty Girl's and Boy's Magic Transformations. Transformation Toy Books Series. New York: McLoughlin Brothers, 1882.
Gift of Herbert H. Hosmer, 1978.

Metamorphic picture books for children date back to the eighteenth century. They usually lacked a narrative and focused instead on silly interchangeable pairings of animal or human bodies. McLoughlin Brothers improved on this format with its Transformation Toy Books Series, which retailed at thirty-five cents each. These colorful books included full stories with the metamorphic images, creating a "before and after" effect that likely delighted readers and non-readers alike. "The Parrot Girl" shows what happens to children who prattle on, not letting others speak—flip the flap and poor Polly has turned into a parrot. Other pages show what happens to children who experiment with smoking or spend too much time looking in the mirror.

171. Heinrich Hoffmann. STREWEL-PETER. New York: McLoughlin Brothers, 1898.

Heinrich Hoffmann's (1809–1894) Slovenly Peter (also called Struwwelpeter or Struwel-Peter) stories were translated from German for the American market around 1850. McLoughlin Brothers issued multiple versions of Hoffmann's cautionary tales, as well as new stories told in a similar style (cat. 89). This volume combines both traditional stories and newer texts. Even during its heyday, McLoughlin Brothers did not overlook demand for traditional stories and rhymes like Struwwelpeter and Mother Goose. These books were constantly updated and enhanced to appeal to changing tastes.

Cat. 171.
Strewel-Peter,
1898.

172. Cinderella or the Little Glass Slipper. Cinderella Series. New York: McLoughlin Brothers, 1897.

Gift of Herbert H. Hosmer, 1978.

The Cinderella Series was among the McLoughlin Brothers output listed in its earliest extant publisher's catalog from 1867 and remained a fixture in the firm's line through 1920. *Cinderella* versions published during the heyday years at the end of the century are often glamourous, large-format affairs, and were designed using a sophisticated palette of shades, as seen in this 1897 edition. The book reflects McLoughlin's commitment to lithography as its chief form of color print technology beginning in 1895. The costumes on Cinderella, the prince, and the footman are historicized, perhaps reflecting the popularity of Edward Burne Jones's designs for *Robin Hood* and Chaucer's *Works* published by William Morris's Kelmscott press in the 1890s.

173. The Owl and the Fox. New York: McLoughlin Brothers, 1896.

Gift of Justin G. Schiller, 2015.

174. Cover design for The Owl and the Fox. Watercolor with gouache, 1896.

Gift of Justin G. Schiller, 2015.

Shaped books were part of the McLoughlin Brothers line from 1858, but really became a staple starting in the 1890s. Classic titles like *Simple Simon*, *Robinson Crusoe* (cat. 129), and *The Owl and the Fox* were produced in this format, along with new stories about Santa Claus (cat. 158) and bicycling. Most were copyrighted by the brothers and all were repurposed into other toys and games, including a bowling set featuring the covers as the pins. Shaped books were made using die-cutting machines powered by steam, which allowed many copies to be produced at once. This was reflected in the price—shaped books were offered as part of the ten-cent book line of the company, putting them in reach of many consumers.

175. Royal Picture Gallery. New York: McLoughlin Brothers, 1894.

Image, pp. 48-49.

176. A.B.C. of Objects for Home and School. Kindergarten First Book. London: Griffith, Farran, Okeden & Welsh. Copyright held by McLoughlin Brothers, 1889.

Gift of Herbert H. Hosmer, 1978.
Image, cover.

During the golden era, McLoughlin Brothers continued to produce products that appealed to a broad age range of readers, from pre-readers to advanced students. These two titles were designed for the youngest children. The sturdy, accordion-bound *Royal Picture Gallery* has no text and unfolds to show six different scenes. The volume was described in McLoughlin's 1895 catalog as extending to thirteen feet with pictures "of peculiar interest to little people."

McLoughlin Brothers also continued to work collaboratively with other publishers when it proved beneficial. The firm partnered with Griffith, Farran, Okeden & Walsh of London, a publisher that produced titles for educational use including craft books, hymnals for Sunday schools, and books for Kindergartens. German immigrants brought the concept of Kindergarten to the United States in the 1850s, and by the 1890s hundreds of schools for young children were operating from Boston to San Francisco. This wordless book, likely printed in Brooklyn by McLoughlin Brothers and distributed to schools around the world from London, features full-page chromolithographed illustrations of animals and objects associated with each letter of the alphabet.

177. YOUNG AMERICA'S A.B.C. AND PRETTY PICTURE BOOK. New York: McLoughlin Brothers, 1899–1900.

Gift of Herbert H. Hosmer, 1978.

178. YANKEE DOODLE ABC AND PICTURE BLOCKS. New York: McLoughlin Brothers, 1899–1900.

Loaned by Richard W. Cheek.

McLoughlin Brothers produced original patriotic titles for over fifty years. At the turn of the century, it continued this tradition with the Young America and Yankee Doodle series, which were full of images of robust American children. With red, white, and blue letters, flags, and patriotic verses, this alphabet picture book was designed to appeal to national pride. Some of the interior illustrations refer to the actions of the recently concluded Spanish-American War (1898), showing that the firm was able to update and refresh its products to keep them relevant to consumers. The large-format, half-bound book was one of the costlier choices available from McLoughlin Brothers in this era, selling retail for $2.50. The ABC blocks feature images on every surface, including alphabet letters, numbers, and toy soldiers, as well as a picture of modern children marching with drum and flag, reminiscent of the popular view of "The Spirit of '76," which appears on the cover of the box.

Cat. 177.
Young America's A.B.C.,
ca. 1899.

179. Parlor Folding Doll House. New York: McLoughlin Brothers, 1894.

Loaned by Richard W. Cheek.

180. Paper Furniture, No. 1. Bedroom Set. New York: McLoughlin Brothers, after 1870.

Over the years, the firm created hundreds of paper toys for children, from dolls to very elaborate "paper amusements" and novelties. In the 1880s, John McLoughlin Jr. filed patents on his doll and paper toy designs to protect them from piracy by his competitors. In 1894 McLoughlin Brothers patented a four-room folding doll house with kitchen, dining room, parlor, and bedroom. The toy was described in the 1896 catalog: "It is designed to be played with on a table. A number of little girls may thus get round it to the very best advantage. It is made of stout binder's board covered with colored designs representing the carpets, walls, windows, mantels, etc." Of course, the company also produced paper furniture to fill the house, stating, "When neatly cut out, this furniture will fit one of our Doll Houses in perfect modern style fit for any family of Dolls in existence."

181. The New Pretty Village. Church Set. New York: McLoughlin Brothers, 1897.

The tabletop toy *The New Pretty Village* was one of the more elaborate paper toys issued by McLoughlin Brothers. It was offered in three models (four buildings, eight buildings, or the whole village with sixteen buildings) and was first released as "The Pretty Village" in 1890. Each set came with paper people, trees, and animals that stood up on metal clips and could be arranged on a paper mat that had the entire plan of the village set out with roads, a river, and farmland. The toy was reviewed by *The American Stationer*: "This delightful amusement is of just that sort in which little children delight, because when busy over it they are, to all intents and purposes, part of the scene itself. . . . It is one of those engaging playthings that children never tire of, and in which their lively fancies have a wide

field for exercise."[28] This set, like the *Parlor Folding Doll House* (cat. 179), can be regarded as the culmination of the paper toy line that began with McLoughlin Brothers penny paper dolls in the 1850s.

182. Animals to Be Cut Out, No. 2. Little Folks Menagerie. New York: McLoughlin Brothers, 1883.

Cut examples loaned by Linda F. and Julian L. Lapides.

Paper toys were always a part of the McLoughlin inventory, from paper dolls and soldiers (cats. 52–54, 190, 191) to foldable furniture (cat. 180). During the golden age of the 1880s and 1890s, the firm also issued multiple sets of paper animals. The figures were printed on heavy stock and varnished with a glittery, eye-catching coating. This set is a mix of wild animals, such as lions and monkeys, with domesticated beasts, such as cows and goats. Although intended primarily for home use, McLoughlin Brothers paper toys and books also made their way into the classroom. The paper animals are mentioned in an 1890 article for educators: "Outline animals, McLoughlin's pictures to cut out: Cut out the animals and distribute to the children for outlining. At the close of the exercise let each child name the animal he has outlined and tell some little fact about its habit of walking, eating, about its peculiarities of form, covering, etc."[29]

Cat. 181. *The New Pretty Village,* 1897.

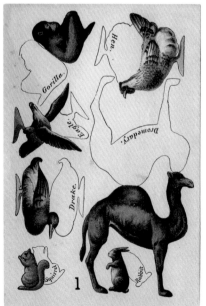

Cat. 182. *Animals to Be Cut Out, No. 2,* 1883.

END OF AN ERA

When John McLoughlin Jr. died in 1905, the strongest driving force behind the company was gone. His brother and cofounder of McLoughlin Brothers, Edmund, had died six years earlier in 1889. John's son Charles, who took the helm after his father's death, passed away in 1914, and his other son, James, had outside pursuits that left him little interest in running the company. Under Charles, the company continued to produce an annual catalog full of old favorites and new titles, and the Brooklyn factory kept humming along. An army of traveling salesmen kept taking orders for classic titles such as *Arabian Nights*, as well as contemporary games featuring popular sports like football and cycling. But the engine that drove the golden years was definitely slowing.

After over fifty years of expansion and experimentation, the firm began to flounder in the years following World War I. Quality dropped as cost-cutting measures introduced inferior pulp paper stock and photomechanically reproduced illustrations. In 1920, the company was sold to the game publisher Milton Bradley in Springfield, Massachusetts. Milton Bradley was primarily interested in the game inventory and patents, many of which were quickly subsumed into its own product line. Bradley retained a diminished version of the book publishing business as well, reissuing some older titles annually, along with a few new books. The art archive, the library of competitors' books, business records, and printing blocks and plates were all moved to Massachusetts, and the factory contents and property in Brooklyn were sold.

A massive flood of the Connecticut River in 1938 filled portions of the Milton Bradley factory with water and likely claimed the McLoughlin Brothers ledgers and business records. The library of books, annual catalogs, and original artwork from the early days were all spared, however, and between 1950 and 1951 these were divided up among several Milton Bradley executives. Much of this material is now preserved in library collections like the American Antiquarian Society and serves as evidence of the processes and procedures used by McLoughlin Brothers during its decades of operation as the largest publisher of juvenile literature in the United States.

Mc Loughlin Bros., Inc.
NEW YORK.
SET-C-0111

Cat. 190.
Paper Dolls,
1915.

183. PARLOR FOOTBALL GAME. New York: McLoughlin Brothers, 1891.

The firm's inventory of novel and attractive games was what attracted Milton Bradley to purchase McLoughlin Brothers in 1920. This eye-catching chromolithographed game box features half of the players wearing the "Y" of the Yale University Bulldogs, while the other half wears the orange and black horizontal jerseys of the Princeton University Tigers. In 1891 when the game was published, the sport of college football was barely more than two decades old, and both Yale and Princeton were among the earliest teams. After 1900, McLoughlin Brothers' product designers capitalized on American children's growing obsession with sports, creating games based on bicycling, rowing, and baseball, to which they would later add automobile racing and aviation.

184. STORY OF THE AMERICAN FIREMAN. New York: McLoughlin Brothers, 1909.

McLoughlin Brothers continued to produce high-quality chromolithographed books after the death of John McLoughlin Jr. in 1905. *Story of the American Fireman* is typical of McLoughlin's best picture book products, overflowing with color plates, bound well with an attractive cover, and full of action designed to appeal to children. Purely American subjects continued to be produced alongside more traditional nursery rhymes and classic tales. This volume was produced just before the circa 1910 decline in overall quality and the adoption of photomechanical halftone plates and pulp-based papers.

185. LOVE'S OFFERING. Valentine, ca. 1900.
Loaned by Linda F. and Julian L. Lapides.

Valentines remained a part of the McLoughlin Brothers business until the transfer to Milton Bradley in 1920. Both comic and sentimental valentines are listed in several of the annual catalogs and occasionally had a catalog of their own as the volume of business required special focus by the sales team. In 1875, McLoughlin and its main valentine competitor, A. J. Fisher, reportedly printed over six million valentines for distribution to markets all over the nation.[30] This moveable card, with snipping scissors, was printed twenty-five years later and shows that the company constantly updated its designs.

Cat. 184. *Story of the American Fireman*, **1909.**

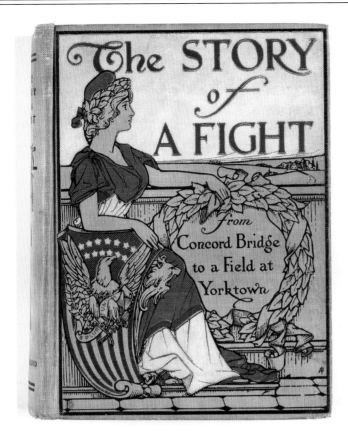

Cat. 186.
The Story of a Fight, 1907.

Antiquarian Society holds the complete file of the original engravings and cyanotypes that were used to create many of the illustrations inside this book, as well as the original pen and ink line art used on the title page and for several interior images. McLoughlin promoted this book heavily during the fall of 1907, saying, "This book is unique, not only in juvenile literature but in historical literature. It supplies a need that every teacher knows exists, and a need which every boy and girl feels unconsciously exists. It is history built on the plan of a story, but it is not historical fiction in any sense. It is what the name suggests, the STORY OF A REAL FIGHT."[31] The quality of production, however, was not up to previous McLoughlin Brothers standards. The paper used was high in pulp content and browned quickly, and the illustrations made with the recently perfected photomechanical process were muddy and indistinct.

186. Hugh Lloyd. THE STORY OF A FIGHT FROM CONCORD BRIDGE TO A FIELD AT YORKTOWN. New York: McLoughlin Brothers, 1907.

187. Title page design from THE STORY OF A FIGHT. Pen and ink, 1907.
Gift of Herbert H. Hosmer, 1978.

188. After Alonzo Chappel. BOSTON MASSACRE. Engraving. New York: Johnson, Fry & Co., 1868.
Gift of Herbert H. Hosmer, 1978.

189. Cyanotype of 1868 BOSTON MASSACRE engraving for reduction in THE STORY OF A FIGHT, 1907.
Gift of Herbert H. Hosmer, 1978.

The book *The Story of a Fight* represents McLoughlin Brothers' attempt to make inroads into the full-length book market for youth under the leadership of Charles McLoughlin, John Jr.'s son. The American

190. PAPER DOLLS, SET C-0111. New York: McLoughlin Brothers, ca. 1915.
Image, pp. 134-135.

191. SOLDIERS ON PARADE. Springfield, Massachusetts: McLoughlin Brothers, 1932.
Loaned by Richard W. Cheek.

McLoughlin Brothers printed paper dolls during its earliest days in the 1850s and continued to do so into the 1940s under Milton Bradley. Many of the firm's classic paper toys, including *The New Pretty Village Toy* (cat. 181), were reprinted over and over again. These paper doll sets show that a variety of paper toys were still being produced by the firm after 1910, and they were marketed to both boys and girls. The sheet of uncut paper dolls includes a suffragette costume with a Votes for Women placard, showing McLoughlin's efforts to adapt its products to current sociopolitical issues. The set of soldiers from 1932 contains multiple pages of uniformed figures with an international flair, including a military band.

192. McLoughlin Bros., Publishers of Toy Books & Juvenile Books, Manufacturers of Paper Dolls, Games, Building and ABC Blocks, Valentines, &c. New York: McLoughlin Brothers, 1871–1874.

Gift of Herbert H. Hosmer, 1978.
Images, endpapers and back cover.

193. McLoughlin Brothers' Catalogue. New York: McLoughlin Brothers, 1895.

Image, p. 144.

194. McLoughlin Brothers Order List. New York: McLoughlin Brothers, 1919.

Gift of Herbert H. Hosmer, 1978.

One of the best ways to trace the business history of McLoughlin Brothers is through the numerous annual catalogs that it published and distributed to resellers and wholesalers across the country. Each product is listed in these volumes, sometimes with pictures and often with wholesale prices given by the gross (144 copies). The earliest surviving catalog of products for the firm is 1867, and over fifty catalogs from that year until 1947 are known. Some of the publications were intended for wholesale customers. Others, like the order lists, were used by salesmen to keep track of business while they were on the road. Because of the complexity of the stock, with similar titles appearing in multiple series and at multiple price points (penny versions and deluxe versions), detailed lists were needed

to keep orders straight. Often McLoughlin Brothers assigned numbers to its products and later used code words that could be sent easily by telegraph.

195. William W. Walker business card, ca. 1900.

Gift of George K. Fox, 2015.

196. Trade cards for the Ten-Dollar Type Writer, A Model Amusement for Girls and Boys, 1884, and for The New and Fashionable Game of Louisa, ca. 1890.

Both gifts of George K. Fox, 2015.

197. The House of Novelties. McLoughlin Books for Children. San Francisco, 1928.

Ephemera, including trade cards and single-sheet advertisements, helps to recreate the story of the firm. Many salesmen traveled extensively for the company. In 1908, a full-page advertisement in *The Publishers' Weekly* named these usually anonymous men: "Our salesmen play no small part in shaping and improving the line. Our men who are off on the road—Black, Kelly, Stephens, Miller, Gilmour, Eckel—and the home guard who look after our friends who call, are optimistic and enthusiastic."[32] The verso of the business card for William Walker, one of the "home guard," includes pre-printed spaces so that Walker could fill in appointment details and then hand the card to a customer.

The two trade cards, which would have been distributed to wholesale customers, feature two very different products: an early precursor to a typewriter from 1884 and a board game from the 1890s. The typewriter card suggests the wide range of products sold by the company. The card for a board game could have been inserted into card games to promote new products or handed out directly to customers.

The single-sheet Kindel & Graham ad promotes the Centennial Line of McLoughlin picture books issued in 1928. This effort was intended to help regenerate consumer interest in the McLoughlin Brothers brand.

Kindel & Graham ran a large toy shop in San Francisco, an excellent venue for McLoughlin's products. The network of resellers established by McLoughlin Brothers in the golden era of 1880 to 1900 expanded after the turn of the century as more independent booksellers and toy shops opened up across the country.

198. ARABIAN NIGHTS. Springfield, Massachusetts: McLoughlin Brothers, after 1920.

199. Unknown artist. "Morgiana with Boiling Oil," from ARABIAN NIGHTS. Watercolor, n.d., late nineteenth century.
Gift of David M. Doret and Linda G. Mitchell, 2016.

The McLoughlin Brothers business archive at the American Antiquarian Society houses several examples of original illustration art used (and reused) during the post-1920 period, after the brand had been sold to Milton Bradley. This image from *Arabian Nights* shows Morgiana about to pour boiling oil into jars in which thieves are hiding. It was created for an edition published before 1900, which was republished in 1912. It was also reused in an anthology published in Springfield after 1920. Changes to the hair of the central figure were being worked out in an attempt to update the drawing. A paste-on of fuller tresses is appended at the upper right for consideration of the editor. The cover of the post-1920 edition used the fuller hair. This reuse and adaptation shows that executives at Milton Bradley continued to dip into the McLoughlin Brothers visual art archives to produce new editions of classic books.

Cat. 199. *Arabian Nights,* **late nineteenth century.**

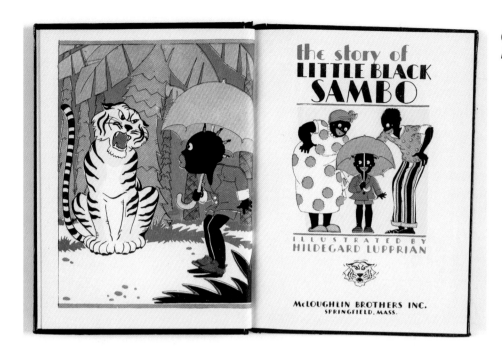

Cat. 200. *The Story of Little Black Sambo*, 1938.

200. Helen Bannermann. THE STORY OF LITTLE BLACK SAMBO. Illustrated by Hildegard Lupprian. Springfield, Massachusetts: McLoughlin Brothers, 1938.
Gift of Herbert H. Hosmer, 1978.

201. OUR AMERICA, LITTLE STORIES FOR YOUNG PATRIOTS. Springfield, Massachusetts: McLoughlin Brothers, 1941.
Gift of Herbert H. Hosmer, 1978.

In an attempt to update the McLoughlin Brothers line for children living in the 1930s and 1940s, the company issued several small-format, affordable books with bold colors and modern illustrations. McLoughlin's 1938 edition of *The Story of Little Black Sambo*, a tale first published in Scotland in 1899, features bright, cartoon-like images made by Philadelphia artist Hildegard Lupprian (b. 1897). This story originally featured a boy from India who successfully negotiates with tigers for his life. It was adapted by American publishers, who made the main character a boy from an undetermined African country, even though no tigers exist on the African continent. The impact of *Little Black Sambo* has been debated by scholars since its publication, with some taking the position that the savvy protagonist empowered children of color, while others find the tale racist and demeaning. The exaggerated facial features of the figures created by Lupprian would have been considered amusing in the 1930s.

Our America, while typical of the type of patriotic picture books published by McLoughlin Brothers for decades, was updated to include 1940s-era scenes and styles of dress. It follows in the tradition of *Yankee Doodle* (cat. 87) and *Young America's A.B.C. and Pretty Picture Book* (cat. 177), both books that celebrated America with images of flag-waving children. Published on the cusp of World War II, *Our America* was one of five titles in the Little Patriotic Library, which featured books such as *The Star-Spangled Banner* and *The Story of Our Navy*. Both *Little Black Sambo* and *Our America* were square-format books quite similar in scale and quality to the popular Little Golden Books series that would debut in 1942.

Cat. 202. *A Birthday Party*, ca. 1920.

202. A BIRTHDAY PARTY AND OTHER STORIES. Springfield, Massachusetts: McLoughlin Brothers, after 1920.

Gift of Herbert H. Hosmer, 1978.

203. Unknown artist. "Cover design with Camp Fire Girls," from A BIRTHDAY PARTY AND OTHER STORIES. Watercolor, pen and ink, after 1920.

Gift of Herbert H. Hosmer, 1978.

This watercolor by an unknown artist idealizes the activities of participants in the newly formed Camp Fire Girls, a group established in New England around 1910. Camp Fire Girls was an organization similar to the Girl Guides and the Girl Scouts, and all three organizations encouraged girls to be active outside, to learn how to navigate in the wilderness, and to work in teams. Most participants in these organizations were white middle-class children, one of the markets sought by McLoughlin Brothers. The firm used this image of girls dressed up in Native American costumes on the cover of a picture book anthology, *A Birthday Party and Other Stories*, published after 1920. By tying the book to the Camp Fire Girls, the firm was showing that it could stay current with trends that would have appealed to many modern girls.

204. Brandon Walsh. Little Annie Rooney Wishing Book. Springfield, Massachusetts: McLoughlin Brothers, 1932.

Gift of Herbert H. Hosmer, 1978.

This book was the result of a 1930s collaboration between the McLoughlin Brothers book line of Milton Bradley and the comics and cartoon publisher King Features Syndicate, established by William Randolph Hearst (1863–1951) in 1914. *Little Annie Rooney* was based on a popular silent movie about a tough Irish girl who was played by America's sweetheart, Mary Pickford (1892–1979). The book is evidence that McLoughlin Brothers continued to use creative marketing relationships into the twentieth century. The arrangement was likely beneficial to both parties— King wanted to get children to go to the movies, and McLoughlin wanted them to buy more books and games. This is one of the earliest uses of crossover marketing between film and book publishing.

205. Geraldyne Clyne [pseudonym for Goldie Jacobs Klein]. "Jack and the Bean Stalk." In The Jolly Jump-Ups Favorite Nursery Stories. Springfield, Massachusetts: McLoughlin Brothers, 1942.

Image, p. 34.

The Jolly Jump-Up pop-up books first appeared in 1939 and featured an American family and their adventures (seeing the circus, going on vacation, buying a house). The series also contained titles for younger children, including an ABC book, a counting book, and this title of nursery rhymes. Many were illustrated by artist Goldie Jacobs Klein (fl. 1939–1948) under the pseudonym Geraldyne Clyne. Klein, the wife of Benjamin Klein, who was an artist and teacher at the Cooper Union in New York, held the copyright to a number of the Jolly Jump-Up books. These books were one of the few strong-selling products issued under the McLoughlin Brothers name after the transfer to Milton Bradley in 1920.

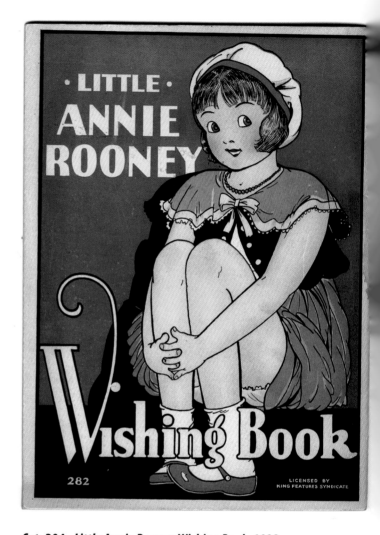

Cat. 204. *Little Annie Rooney Wishing Book,* **1932.**

EARLY HISTORY OF PICTURE BOOKS IN AMERICA

1. Pierre Samuel Du Pont de Nemours, *National Education in the United States of America*, 1923 translation of 1812 second Paris edition (Wilmington: University of Delaware, 1923): 3.

CHILDREN'S BOOK PUBLISHING IN NEW YORK

2. "Catalogue of the Fall Trade Sale," *American Publishers' Circular and Literary Gazette* 2, no. 34 (August 25, 1856): 503.
3. "For Juveniles," *Boston Evening Transcript*, October 25, 1858, 1.
4. *O'Brien's Philadelphia Wholesale Business Directory* (Philadelphia: King & Baird, 1844): 51.
5. "Catalogue of the Fall Trade Sale," 502.

EARLY DAYS OF MCLOUGHLIN BROTHERS

6. "Children's Books," *Brooklyn Daily Eagle*, December 22, 1866, 2.
7. "Catalogue of the Fall Trade Sale," 501–503. This tally does not include publishers of school books.
8. *The Bookseller: The Organ of the Book Trade*, December 6, 1862, 861.

ILLUSTRATORS AT MCLOUGHLIN BROTHERS

9. See Barbara J. Balliet, "Let Them Study as Men and Work as Women," *Common-place* 7, no. 3 (April 2007), http://common-place.org/book/let-them-study-as-men-and-work-as-women/.
10. "New Books from Rand McNally and Co.," *The Publishers' Weekly* 84, no. 2180 (November 15, 1913): 1558.

DIFFICULTIES OF NINETEENTH-CENTURY HUMOR

11. See *The American Stationer* 12 (October 12, 1882): 568.
12. Elizabeth Stordeur Pryor, "The N-Word in the Antebellum North: Subversive Readings of the Visual Archive" (seminar lecture, *In Black and White: Race in American Visual Culture*, Center for Historic American Visual Culture, American Antiquarian Society, Worcester, MA, June 12, 2017).

MCLOUGHLIN BROTHERS AND ITS COMPETITORS

13. "An American Pasternoster Row," *The Publishers' Weekly* 43, no. 1103 (March 18, 1893): 454–455.
14. *McLoughlin Brothers Fifty-Fifth Annual Catalogue of Paper and Linen Toy Books* . . . (New York: McLoughlin Brothers, 1903). San Francisco Public Library.
15. "Dean & Son List of New Books," *The Bookseller, A Handbook of British and Foreign Literature* 22 (October 26, 1859): 1309.
16. Robert J. Buck, *Trail Blazers of the Thomson Gamble Family* (Asheville, NC: Reuben B. Robertson, 1948): 15.
17. "The Fall Trade," *The Publishers' Weekly* 20, no. 504–505 (September 17, 1881): 281.
18. "E. P. Dutton & Co., and Raphael Tuck & Sons Co. Charged with Violating the Copyright Law," *The Publishers' Weekly* 50, no. 1281 (August 15, 1896): 235. See also "The Copyright issue," *The American Stationer* 40 (August 27, 1896): 337. The case was heard by the U.S. Circuit Court of the Southern District of New York. See also *Treasury Decisions under Customs and Other Laws*, vol. 29 (Washington: Government Printing Office, 1916): 808–810.

MCLOUGHLIN BROTHERS' STEADY SELLERS

19. "Individual Book Exhibits," *The Publishers' Weekly* 10, no. 233 (July 1, 1876): 23.
20. "Galaxy Advertiser," *The Galaxy* 10 (December 1870): 20.
21. *The American Stationer* 18 (October 29, 1885): 549.
22. *Christianity Practically Applied. The Discussions of the International Christian Conference* (Chicago: Baker & Taylor, 1894): 259.
23. "Juvenile Books for the Holidays," *The American Bookseller* 30 (November 21, 1891): 292.

THE GOLDEN AGE OF MCLOUGHLIN BROTHERS

24. "The House of McLoughlin Brothers in 1908," *The Publishers' Weekly* 73, no. 1883 (February 29, 1908): 980.
25. Charles A. B. Shepard, "Forty Years' Progress in Juveniles," *The Publishers' Weekly* 29, no. 745 (May 8, 1886): 599.
26. See advertisement on back cover of *Cinderella and the Little Glass Slipper, Little Plays for Little Players* (New York: McLoughlin Brothers, 1883). Harvard University.
27. "Trade Items," *The American Stationer* 30 (November 5, 1891): 969.
28. *The American Stationer* 28 (October 9, 1890): 877.
29. "Busy Work Exercises," *The American Primary Teacher* 13 (May 1890): 334.

END OF AN ERA

30. "Valentines for the Virtuous and Vicious," *The Publishers' Weekly* 3, no. 157 (January 16, 1875): 60.
31. *The Publishers' Weekly* 72, no. 1861 (September 28, 1907): 914.
32. "The House of McLoughlin Brothers in 1908," 980.

Colophon

Radiant with Color & Art: McLoughlin Brothers and the Business of Picture Books, 1858–1920 was published in November 2017.

The text is set in Myriad and Minion and is printed on Endurance.

Printed in four-color process by Puritan Capital Inc. in Hollis, New Hampshire, and bound by Optimum Bindery in Nashua, New Hampshire.

Design elements—including type size, leading, column width, title caps, size, page numbers, and bar use—were inspired by the original McLoughlin Brothers publishers' catalogs printed between the 1870s and the 1940s.

Cat. 193. *McLoughlin Brothers' Catalogue*, 1895.

Cat. 67. *A Peep at Buffalo Bill's Wild West, 1887.*

1 Dozen	Aunt Jenny's Series	Retail 15cts. each,		$1 80
1 "	" " Musical Series	" 15	"	1 80
1 "	Mamma Lovechild's Series	" 15	"	1 80
1 "	Aunt Oddamadodd	" 15	"	1 80
1 "	Gilt Cover Series. (New)	" 20	"	2 40
1 "	Aunt Mary Series. 8vo	" 20	"	2 40
1 "	Golden Light " (New)	" 20	"	2 40
1 "	Half Hours with the Bible. No. 1	" 15	"	1 80
1 "	" " " " " No. 2 (New)	" 15	"	1 80
1 "	Great Big A B C	" 15	"	1 80
1 "	Aunt Matilda Series	" 20	"	2 40
1 "	Aunt Lulu "	" 20	"	2 40
1 "	Goody-Two-Shoes Series	" 20	"	2 40
1 "	Linen Books. Reduced Price	" 20	"	2 40
1 "	Child's First Book	" 20	"	2 40
1 "	" Home A B C	" 20	"	2 40
1 "	Jack Spraggles Comic His. of Robinson Crusoe	20	"	2 40
1 "	Aunt Louisa. (All New)	" 25	"	3 00
1 "	Favorite Series. Stiff Covers. Price reduced	25	"	3 00
1 "	Mother Goose. Plain. 96 pages	" 25	"	3 00
1 "	Mrs. Hale's Library. Boards	" 25	"	3 00
1 "	Dame Dingle. Stiff Covers	" 25	"	3 00
1 "	Mother Goose. Colored. 96 pages	" 40	"	4 80
1 "	" " Cut out. (New). Price reduced	12	"	1 44
½ "	Uncle Cefil's Story Books. Stiff Covers	" 50	"	3 00
½ "	Old Nurse " " "	" 50	"	3 00
½ "	Mother Goose. Set to Music. (New)	" 50	"	3 00
½ "	Goody-Two-Shoes Story Books. Stiff Covers	" 1.00	"	6 00
1 "	Fashion Series of Paper Dolls	" 25	"	3 00

$102 72

The above Lot, amounting to $102.72, at retail, will be sent on receipt of $50.00.

$100 Lot of Toy Books,

Games, Paper Dolls, Building, A B C and Spelling Blocks, Panoramas,

&c., &c., &c.

☞ This Lot comprises an entire line of our publications and manufactures, amounting to $117.75, at wholesale prices.

This Lot we send on receipt of $100.

BOUND JUVENILES.

¼ Dozen	Goody-Two-Shoes	Retailing at $1 00 each.		$3 00
¼ "	Uncle Cefil's Story Book	" " 50	"	1 50
¼ "	Old Nurse's Book	" " 50	"	1 50
1 "	Mrs. Hale's Library	" " 25	"	3 00
½ "	Dame Dingles' Series	" " 25	"	1 50
½ "	Favorite Series	" " 25	"	1 50
½ "	Robinson Crusoe, in one Syllable,	" " 75	"	4 50

$16 50

The above are very neatly bound in stiff board covers, and will give a very fair assortment. We will send it on receipt of $10.00.

Sample Lot of Panoramas.

3 Nursery Panoramas	at 30 cts. each,		$0 90
2 Little Pet "	50	"	1 00
1 Major's "	50	"	50
1 Negro Minstrel Panorama			1 50
1 Menagerie "			1 50
1 Uncle Sam's "			1 50
1 Humpty Dumpty "			1 50

$8 40

The above Lot of Panoramas are the most desirable and saleable articles you could have. They are very large size, and have 12 beautiful Illustrations in oil colors, which, when shown in a dark room, with a light behind them, is far superior to any Magic Lantern. Will be sent on receipt of $5.00.

One Cent Books—Dolls and Games.

Little Dot Series. Books		Per Gross,		$1 00
Aunt Grumble "		"	"	"
Little Pleasewell "		"	"	"
" Delights "		"	"	"
Aunt Mary's Little Series		"	"	"
Young America		"	"	"
Penny Soldiers. In Boxes. Assorted		"	"	"
" Animals. Very funny. In Boxes. Assorted		"	"	"
Gem Series. New		"	"	"
Tom Thumb. 2 Dolls in one. New		"	"	"

Penny Games. Each game complete in itself. Printed in colors.
Per Gross, 1 00

Slate Drawing Books. Something new, and the best thing ever published for children. Well assorted. Per Gross, 1 50

$5 Lot of Paper Dolls.

50	No. 1. Paper Dolls. 22 kinds.	5 cents each			$2 50
24	" 2. " "	24 "	10	"	2 40
12	" 3. " "	12 "	15	"	1 80
12	" 3. " " New 3 "	15	"	1 80
6	Dressed. " " "	25	"	1 50

$10 00

The above Lot, amounting to $10.00, at retail, will be sent on receipt of $5.00.

$10 Lot of Paper Dolls.

5	No. 1. Paper Dolls. 22 kinds.	5 cents each			$2 50
48	" 2. " "	24 "	10	"	4 80
24	" 3. " "	12 "	15	"	3 60
16	" 3. " " New 3 "	15	"	2 40
20	" 4. " "	4 "	20	"	4 00
12	Dressed " " New.		25	"	3 00

$20 30

The above Lot, amounting to $20.30, at retail, will be sent on receipt of $10.00.

$5 Lot of Games.

72 Games. Assorted. 6 kinds	at 1 cent each,			$0 72
12 Large Games. 12 "	37½	"		4 50
6 Cinderella Series of Games. 6 kinds	25	"		1 50
6 New Games. 6 kinds	25	"		1 50

$8 22

This assortment comprises 30 different Games, all of them very desirable. We will send it on receipt of $5.00.

$10 Lot of Games.

6 Dozen	Games	at 1 cent each,		$0 72
1 "	Large Games. 12 kinds	37½ "		4 50
1 "	Home " 12 "	25 "		3 00
1 "	Cinderella Series of Games. 6 kinds	25 "		3 00
1½ "	Dissected Pictures. 18 kinds	25 "		4 50
¼ "	Old Maid Game	25 "		75
¼ "	Dr. Fusby	25 "		75

$17 22

The above Lot comprises 60 different kinds of Games, and contains the very best kinds we publish. We will send it on receipt of $10.00.

$5.00 SAMPLE LOT OF
SUNDAY-SCHOOL BOOKS & REWARDS.

4 Dozen	Watts' Songs	Retail at 5cts. each,		$2 40
1 "	Bible Stories. No. 1	" 15	"	1 80
1 "	" " 2. (New)	" 15	"	1 80
1 "	Golden Light. (New)	" 20	"	2 40
1½ "	Illuminated Texts. Very fine	" 15	"	2 70

$11 10

This Lot, amounting to $11.10, at retail, will be sent on receipt of $5.00.

SAMPLE LOT OF
A B C BLOCKS, SPELLING BLOCKS,
AND THE WONDERFUL
SWIFT COMBINATION BUILDING BLOCKS.

2 Boxes A B C Blocks		at 25 cts each,	$0 50
1 Box Goody-Two-Shoes Spelling Blocks			1 00
1 " " " " "			1 50
1 " " " " "			2 00
1 " Building Blocks			1 00
1 " " "			1 50
1 " " "			2 50
1 " " "			5 00
			$15 00

The above Blocks are all new and of the most approved styles, and very salable. The Building Blocks are the finest ever invented ; they are made of Rock Maple, and each set put up in a fine Wood Box. This Lot will be sent on receipt of $10.00.

CUT TISSUE PAPER.

We have constantly on hand a large variety of Cut Tissue Paper, for trimming Picture and Looking Glass Frames, and for Decorating Ceilings. Also Shelf Paper, different patterns, and all colors.

FRAME PAPER.

No. 1, 2½ inches wide		$1.50 per dozen pieces.
" 2, 5 " "		3.00 " "
" 3, 7½ " "		4.50 " "
" 4, 10 " "		6.00 " "

All colors, 25 yards in each piece.
Ceiling Paper, in assorted quires....25cts. per quire, or $4.00 per ream.
Shelf Paper, all colors... $1.80 per gross sheets.

NOW READY.
DICKENS' CHRISTMAS STORY.
"THE GOBLINS WHO STOLE A SEXTON,"
WITH 26 ILLUSTRATIONS BY THOMAS NAST.

This is one of the best of Dicken's Stories, and will be read with pleasure by old and young. The Illustrations, alone, are worth many times the price of the Book. Price $1.25 per dozen.

BOOKS IN PACKAGES.

One Cent Toys.

Little Dot Series. New.	9 kinds	Per Gross,	$1 00
Aunt Grumble Series "	9 "	" "	1 00
Little Pleasewell Series "	9 "	" "	1 00
" Delights "	9 "	" "	1 00
Young America "	6 "	" "	1 00
Aunt Mary's Little "	12 "	" "	1 00
" " " Primer	1 "	" "	1 00

Two Cent Toys.

Easy Pictures for Slate Drawing. 6 kinds	Per Gross,	$1 50

Five Cent Toys.

Dr. Watts' Songs.	6 kinds	Per Dozen,	$0 25
Uncle Frank Series	12 "	" "	25
Pleasure Books	6 "	" "	25
Uncle Pepin's	6 "	" "	25
Golden A B C	1 "	" "	25
Little Pet's Primer	1 "	" "	25

Six Cent Toys.

Mother's Series.	6 kinds	Per Dozen,	$0 37½
Father's "	"	" "	37½

Eight Cent Toys.

Susie Sunshine	6 kinds	Per Dozen,	$0 37½
Fairy Moonbeam	6 "	" "	37½
Peter Prim	6 "	" "	37½
Slovenly Peter	6 "	" "	37½
Dame Wonder	12 "	" "	37½
Aunt Effie	12 "	" "	37½
Good Boy's Primer	1 "	" "	37½
Good Girl's "	1 "	" "	37½
Nursery A B C	1 "	" "	37½
Major's "	1 "	" "	37½
Aunt Mavors	12 "	" "	50
Willie Winkie	12 "	" "	50
Aunt Busy Bee	6 "	" "	50

Ten Cent Toys.

Æsop's Fables.	12 kinds	Per Dozen,	$0 63
Nursery Series	6 "	" "	63
Nursery Apple Pie	1 "	" "	63
Aunt Friendly Series	6 "	" "	63

Twelve Cent Toys.

Cinderella Series.	6 kinds	Per Dozen,	$0 75
Uncle Cefil "	6 "	" "	75
Dame Dingle "	6 "	" "	75
Joyful Tales "	6 "	" "	75
Natural History	6 "	" "	75
Miss Merryheart	6 "	" "	75
Home Primer	1 "	" "	75
Aunt Lely Alphabet	1 "	" "	75
Story of an Apple Pie	1 "	" "	75

Fifteen Cent Toys.

Mamma Lovechild.	6 kinds	Per Dozen,	$0 87
Aunt Jenny	6 "	" "	87
" Oddamadodd	12 "	" "	87
Papa's Stories	6 "	" "	87
Musical Stories	6 "	" "	87
Union Toys	6 "	" "	1 00

Twenty Cent Toys.

Aunt Mary, 8vo.	12 kinds	Per Dozen	$1 00
Pleasure Books	12 "	" "	1 00
Bible Stories, 1st Series	6 "	" "	1 00
" " 2d "	6 "	" "	1 00
Golden Light	6 "	" "	1 00
Great Big A B C	1 "	" "	1 00
Child's First Book	1 "	" "	1 00
Picture Alphabet	1 "	" "	1 00
Darling's A B C	1 "	" "	1 00
Child's Home A B C	1 "	" "	1 00
Mayflower Picture Alphabet	1 "	" "	1 00
Arthur's Alphabet	1 "	" "	1 00
Gilt Covers. New.	4 "	" "	1 00
Stories of Animals, new	12 "	" "	1 00
Aunt Matilda. New.	6 "	" "	1 25
" Fanny Fairy Tales	12 "	" "	1 25
Mrs. Elliott's Stories	6 "	" "	1 25
Jack Spraggles' Robinson Crusoe	1 "	" "	1 25
Alphabet of Animals	1 "	" "	1 25
Aunt Lulu Series	6 "	" "	1 50
Goody-Two-Shoes	6 "	" "	1 50
Aunt Kitty's	6 "	" "	1 50
Shadows on the Wall	1 "	" "	1 50

Miscellaneous.

Mother Goose. Old Style			$0 37½
" " 16mo			1 00
" " Cut out Shape of the Old Lady. *Price Reduced.*			75
" " Quarto. Plain		Per Dozen,	2 00
" " " Colored			3 00
" " " " Flexible Cov. "			4 50
Nursery Rhymes. 4to. Plain			2 00
" " " Colored			3 00
" " " Flexible Covers "			4 50

Twenty-Five Cent Toys.
Printed in Oil Colors. Six Beautiful Illustrations.

Visit to the Menagerie. Royal 4to		Per Dozen,	$2 00
Domestic Animals "		" "	2 00
Home Games for Boys "		" "	2 00
" " " Girls "		" "	2 00
Tom Thumb "		" "	2 00
Three Bears "		" "	2 00
Yankee Doodle "		" "	2 00

PAINTING BOOK
YOUNG ARTIST
DRAWINGS BY W. BRUTON

Cat. 150. William
Bruton, *Young Artist
Painting Book,* ca.
1882

McLOUGHLIN·BROTHERS·NEW·YORK·